the
Sea
Lover's
Cookbook

the Sea Lover's Cookbook

Recipes for Memorable Meals On or Near the Water

SIDNEY BENSIMON

CHRONICLE BOOKS
SAN FRANCISCO

Library of Congress Cataloging-in-Publication Data available.

ISBN 978-1-7972-0597-7

Manufactured in China.

MIX
Paper | Supporting responsible forestry
FSC™ C008047

Photography by **Sidney Bensimon**.
Recipe development by **Laura Motley**.
Food styling by **Pearl Jones**, **Laura Motley**, and **Sidney Bensimon**.
Prop styling by **Rebecca Bartoshesky** and **Sidney Bensimon**.
Design by **Lizzie Vaughan**.
Typesetting by **Taylor Roy**.
Typeset in Albra, Causten Round, and Swell.

10 9 8 7 6 5 4 3 2 1

Chronicle books and gifts are available at special quantity discounts to corporations, professional associations, literacy programs, and other organizations. For details and discount information, please contact our premiums department at corporatesales@chroniclebooks.com or at 1-800-759-0190.

Chronicle Books LLC
680 Second Street
San Francisco, California 94107
www.chroniclebooks.com

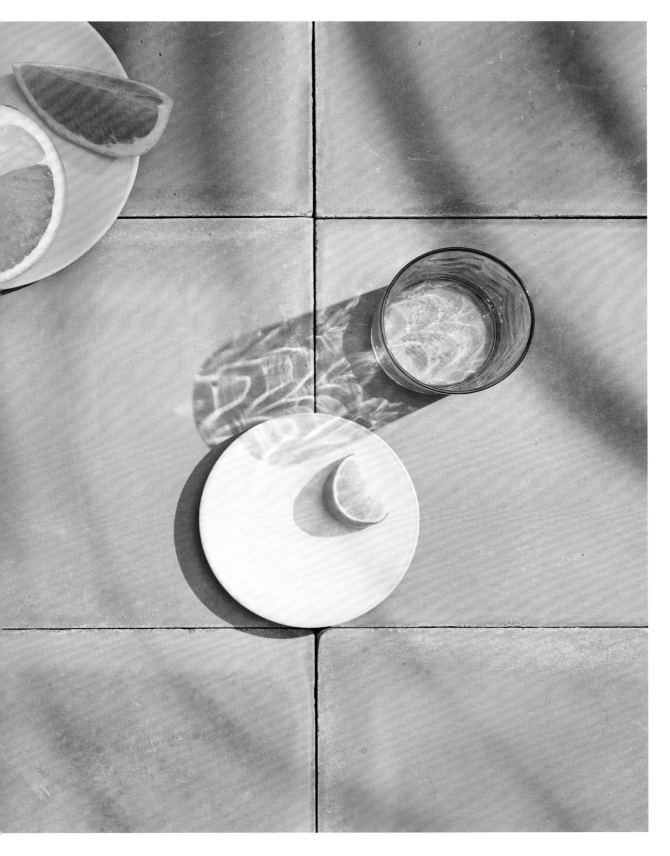

Contents

Introduction

My Story

The Sea Lover's Cookbook was born from my love of the sea and my love of cooking with others. My fondest childhood memories are of summers spent on the beaches of Corsica. My family would rent an apartment right on the beach in a little town near Bonifacio. Every day, all the children in town would meet on the beach to play—whether or not we spoke the same language. In the morning, we would go on boat rides and take turns getting pulled on an inflatable device behind the boat. In the afternoons, we would play in the water, collect rocks and shells, tell stories in the shade, and look for dolphins. I can't remember all the details as much as I remember feeling free.

As I grew up, a passion for photography turned into a career, and I began to shoot for food publications and cookbooks. A photography job took me to Croatia for a week on a boat with the Sailing Collective, a company that charters private voyages all over the world. My job was to photograph the trips. I could swim whenever I wanted! If the boat was anchored, I was jumping in. I loved the constant, gentle rocking of the boat, the feeling of being cradled by the sea. I fell in love with the whole experience. I was, as they say, hooked on sailing, and I wanted more.

I joined the company for a few years, working as a photographer and cooking whenever I had time to step out of my commercial photography business. I sailed to the coasts of Italy, Martinique, Haiti, Thailand, Greece, Croatia, and the British Virgin Islands. On these trips, I was joined by families, strangers, and friends. I learned that no matter how different you are from someone else, there is always common ground to be found, conversations to have, and laughs to share. People from all walks of life share a love for the sea and a love of food, and that is sometimes enough to inspire a friendship.

Full disclosure: I am neither a sailor nor a trained chef. But after about ten sailing trips around the world, cooking for people I knew and didn't know, I found myself comfortable in the kitchen—and I was content. I would get inspired thinking about what to cook next. Mealtimes brought captain, crew, and passengers together. Like many home cooks, I think cooking is a way not only to serve others and make people happy but to stay creative, get out of your head, and make things happen.

On those journeys, I learned to cook in the smallest galleys (a.k.a. boat kitchens), use whatever supplies we had on board, and draw inspiration from the surrounding water and local beaches. Meals were really fun for me to troubleshoot—for example, if I ran out of an ingredient or if I didn't have certain tools I needed, like a blender. Cooking forced me to think creatively. In a galley, you need to be more cautious than in a regular kitchen and to slow down all your movements. A wave can cause you to lose your balance, and staying safe is most important. It's nice to have a reason to slow down, whether or not you're on a boat. Slow cooking is pure pleasure.

Once, in Greece, I wanted to make Greek yogurt ice cream. I tried to think of a way to make that without an ice cream maker. We placed Greek yogurt, local honey, and Maldon sea salt in a Ziploc bag and put it in another bag filled with ice. We tied the bag with a thick rope and tossed it in the waves. My idea was that the movement of the water would churn the yogurt into ice cream. As you might've guessed, it was a big failure—but a fun experiment that I'll never forget. I have so many memories like this. Part of the fun of cooking is making food your own way, and I hope that you allow yourself to experience that, with the recipes in this book and beyond, and in whatever location you find yourself.

My cooking didn't stop in the galley. I still cook at home for my little family and my friends. To this day, creating nourishing meals for myself and others is one of my favorite things to do—and all the better if I can do it by the sea.

My life is very different now than it was when I used to sail. I still enjoy day trips when I have time, but being a professional photographer, owning a business, being a new mom, and, well, just life on top of all that mean that weeklong sailing trips don't happen all that often. I look forward to the time when my family and I can embark on longer sailing trips again—I can't wait to share that experience with my husband, Devin, and my sweet daughter, Romy. In the meantime, I still cook these recipes at home to remind me of the water.

This Book

My taste buds have always been intuitive, and I can really sense if food has been prepared with love. Of course, the fresher, the tastier! I believe that if you have respect for where your food is coming from and the history of its journey, it tastes better and is easier to digest. My extensive travels have continued to prove this to be true, and in this book, I share many of my own guidelines and tips for finding the best produce, products, and wines, no matter your port of call. I will share how I shop, cook, and eat when I am sailing on my boat or traveling in a foreign place. You can also apply these practices if you're simply cooking at home and dreaming of the sea.

To me, the ocean has a personality. It is often calm and sweet in the morning; by midday, it has lots of energy and wants to play; and when dusk sets in, it's restful and romantic. I feel my best when my body beats to the same drum, and I've organized this book by these moods and moments. The chapters here take their cues from the time of day: mornings, midday, and sunset.

I am *imagining* you taking this book on your vacations, *by the beach, on a boat, in a bungalow.* I hope this cookbook travels with you wherever your *adventures* take you, and can help you *ground yourself,* one meal at a time, making you and your loved ones *feel at home anywhere* in the world.

The sea is still one of my favorite places to be. I wrote this cookbook to share with you my passion for the water, as well as the recipes I have come to love over time. I hope you feel inspired to create your own memories of adventures and wonderful meals shared with loved ones. Most important, I invite you to stay curious and have fun.

One Last Note

When I was eight months pregnant, my husband and I were hiking one of my favorite trails in mid-coast Maine, where we have a home. We were standing on big rocks above the ocean, staring out at the water. "What is more beautiful and multifaceted than the ocean? Do you love anything more?" I asked him. "Not much," he said, and I agree. (In fact, our mutual love for the ocean is how we came up with our daughter's middle name, Océane.)

So, my fellow sea lovers, my wish for you is more adventures on the water, wind in your hair, and salt on your skin. More sunrises viewed from the shoreline, coffee in hand, as the waves lap at your feet. More sundowns sipping on cocktails, and more evenings on deck under the starry night sky. And lots more meals of briny seafood, vegetables grilled over open flames, salty snacks, and crisp white wine shared with friends and family along the coast. I hope this book inspires you to adventure both on and near the water, and to get in the kitchen to enjoy these recipes.

Happy sailing and happy cooking! ■

The ingredients in these recipes are easy to swap out depending on what is available at home or during your travels. One only needs the humblest of kitchens—a heat source, a sharp knife, and good ingredients—to re-create these recipes. A few recipes are more easily made with a blender, and others require a bit of prep time; make sure you read them all the way through before you set out on your journey.

You don't need to be on a sailboat to appreciate or cook these recipes, either. This book is not solely for the sailors out there but for anyone who loves Mother Nature, the sea, traveling, and experiencing different cultures through taste. A love for the ocean can come through in your cooking, no matter where you are.

Provisioning, or Stocking
Your Seaside Pantry

Provisioning well is the key to a successful food experience on a boat. What I mean by provisioning is gathering all your food supplies as well as everyday necessities (such as toilet paper, water, sustainable dish soap, etc.), and stocking your boat before you set sail.

When it comes to good supplies, I find it's imperative that I make a list before my trip, otherwise I'll inevitably forget something. I usually separate my list into pantry ingredients, fresh ingredients, water, and other needs. I also like to have a loose meal plan to follow. Alongside each meal, I'll write down the ingredients needed and create a shopping list from there. That way, with a little organization, I can plan for success in the kitchen.

I recommend dedicating two days to building up your onboard stores: one day for dried goods and nonperishables, and one day to gather all the fresh produce you will need. If you can plan for your boat to leave the day after the farmers' market near your dock, then you are impressive!

Make a general list of ingredients, and include more specific items you will need if you choose to cook recipes from this book. Keep in mind that you might feel inspired as you shop too. By planning your meals ahead, you can make sure to use food that wilts the fastest first, while keeping the more robust produce for later on in the week. Root vegetables such as beets, potatoes, and carrots can last a few weeks, but delicate leaves like little gems, mixed greens, and herbs wilt quickly.

I have only shopped for a week's worth of food at most for my trips, but the number of people to cook for has varied. I would suggest buying fresh produce to last a week, and then buying additional complementary fresh ingredients when you make stops throughout the voyage. For example, if you are docking on land or strolling around a town and come across a fresh food stand or market on your adventures, pop in and replenish your fresh ingredient items.

Remember that sailing is like camping on the water, and whatever you take with you, you will mostly bring back, so be aware of the little things. Use reusable packaging whenever possible to minimize your trash. This also goes for when you are renting a place by the beach! Any time you travel, shopping efficiently and avoiding plastic-wrapped ingredients should be a priority. ∎

The Essentials

Here are the must-have items for any sailing or beach trip. You can also find a checklist that's useful for packing on page 23.

Beans: Black beans, pinto beans, white beans, dried beans, canned beans—all beans are great. They store perfectly. Soak dried beans overnight before cooking; simply rinse canned beans before using.

Chips: Get lots of chips! It's such an easy snack to munch on, and the salt can help with boat nausea.

Coffee: There's nothing worse than bad coffee to start the day. I am a coffee snob, so I used to travel with my favorite artisanal beans and a hand grinder. However, since having a baby, I pre-grind my beans before a trip. Do whatever is best for yourself. No judgment here!

Corn tortillas: Unless you are in an area where tortillas are common, I feel like good tortillas are hard to find. I purchase a big pack before my trip since they travel well and last a while at room temperature in the shade. You can use them for breakfast tacos or Fish Tacos (page 154), or fry them up at the end of your trip for a nacho platter topped with Guacamole (page 113).

Dried pasta: Short, long, get them all. Pasta is easy to store and lasts forever. I like to purchase bucatini if I can find it, penne since it holds sauces so well, and classic elbow pasta.

Fats: When shopping for dried goods, go all out on really good-quality **olive oil** and **coconut oil**. Both these oils keeps really well, even if you are traveling to warm places. The coconut oil might become liquid if it gets too hot, but not to worry, it still works wonders. These fats, and of course **butter**, will be your fat base for most dishes. I am not shy in using a copious amount of fat in all my cooking, so I usually get a big container of each—at least 25 oz [740 ml] for olive oil and two 8 oz [230 g] sticks of butter. A jar of coconut oil will suffice.

Nuts and dried fruit: Go nuts on nuts and dried fruit. These are easy snacks for everyone to munch on throughout the day, especially with an aperitif in hand. I particularly love using pistachios in my cooking.

Spices: In preparation for a trip, I like to fill small 1 cup [240 ml] mason jars with my preferred spices. I always bring a jar of **Maldon salt**, a jar of high-quality **red pepper flakes**, and some **dried herbs**. I also have two spice mixes that I like to make ahead of my trip and take with me, a savory and a sweet:

Savory spice mix: Equal parts high-quality ground turmeric, coriander, curry, cumin, and ginger. Use this as an easy seasoning on boiled beans, a curry dish, or sautéed greens.

Sweet spice mix: Equal parts high-quality ground turmeric, cinnamon, and ginger, brown sugar, a pinch of salt, and a dash of black pepper. Use this for the Warm Turmeric Latte with coconut milk (page 37) or the Turmeric Oatmeal (page 47), or to spice up morning pancakes or a simple cake.

Sweeteners: Great bets include **honey** and **coconut sugar**. Try to get local honey if you can.

Other dried and canned goods: I like to keep various dry goods on hand, including staples such as **rice** and **oats**, as well as snacky bites that can round out a lunch, like high-quality **tuna** in olive oil, or complement a cocktail, like **olives**. If any canned items haven't been used up by the end of the trip, I like to pass them on to the next guests.

Bread: Get fresh bread from the market if you can. I always go for a local **sourdough** and I like to have it pre-sliced, as not all boats and vacation homes have a good serrated knife to cut bread.

Water: Do the calculation beforehand and purchase 1 gal [3.8 L] of water per person per day. So if you are a group of six going on a five-day journey, you should buy at least 30 gal [114 L] of drinking water. Unfortunately, it is the only safe way I know to drink water on a boat, but I really wish there was another way, because at the end of a trip, the amount of water-bottle recycling makes my stomach turn. If you can try to find more sustainable packaging, please do.

Dairy: In most European countries, there are stores dedicated to dairy, such as cheese shops. In France, the yogurt aisle is out of control! Every time I go back to France, it's like Christmas when I shop for yogurt and cheese. It's always nice to lean into the cultural cuisine of the place you are traveling to, such as getting stracciatella in Italy, feta in Greece, and paneer in India. **Parmesan** is a crowd-pleaser and stores better than soft cheeses. Dairy, in most cases, needs to be refrigerated, so make sure the fridge is working properly and check it throughout your trip in case it gives out. Sometimes when you overfill a fridge, it doesn't work as well, so be mindful of that—no one wants to get sick on vacation.

Seafood: I recommend purchasing fish and cooking it that day or the next. If you want to cook fish on a later day of the trip, I highly suggest purchasing it closer to the time you want to cook it. Go to your local fishmonger if you can or buy organic at the grocery store.

Vegetables and fruits: As a general rule, opt for produce that doesn't require refrigeration—**stone fruits, root vegetables, bananas, sweet potatoes, mushrooms, onions**, etc. None of these need to be refrigerated, allowing you to save some space in your small fridge in the galley (or kitchen) for items that absolutely require refrigeration, such as berries, tender greens, dairy, and meats.

I once brought a bunch of bananas on a boat, and my captain for the week was very upset with me. She told me it was bad luck to bring a bunch of bananas on a boat! (The reason for this superstition is because bananas can cause other fruits to spoil faster. Superstitions in boating are a *thing*!) That said, I love bananas, so if you want to bring them, just keep them separate from other fruits (and maybe check with your captain first).

Lemons and **limes** last all week on a boat, so don't be shy and pile them in your galley. You will use them every day—for seasoning, salad dressing, and drinking water. If you have leftover citrus, make margaritas or lemonade for the last night of your trip.

Pack in Advance: Your Chef's Kit

Well before a trip, I like to pack a small bag of cooking essentials to take with me—a.k.a., a chef's kit. Some of the best advice I was given was to travel with my favorite spices and one good knife—and by *good*, I mean sharp! Your chef's kit will go a long way toward making meal prep feel simpler and familiar. My chef's kit contains: **one medium, very sharp chef's knife; a general Microplane for zesting; my favorite coffee beans; Maldon salt;** and **my spice mixes** (see page 20).

Provisions Checklist

Here is an example of one of my provisions lists—you can use this as a checklist when packing. Purchase amounts that are appropriate for the number of people you are cooking for.

Pantry

- [ ] White vinegar
- [ ] Apple cider vinegar
- [ ] Olive oil
- [ ] Coconut oil
- [ ] Coconut milk
- [ ] Almond butter
- [ ] Tahini
- [ ] Nutella
- [ ] Honey
- [ ] Mustard
- [ ] Vegetable broth
- [ ] Fish sauce
- [ ] Brown sugar
- [ ] Vanilla extract
- [ ] All-purpose flour
- [ ] Salt and pepper
- [ ] Maldon salt
- [ ] Ground cumin
- [ ] Red pepper flakes
- [ ] Cashews, walnuts, pistachios
- [ ] Dried fruits
- [ ] Granola (store-bought, or make the recipe on page 44 ahead of time)
- [ ] Oatmeal
- [ ] Rice
- [ ] Pasta

- [ ] Dried beans
- [ ] Canned chickpeas
- [ ] Sourdough bread
- [ ] Corn tortillas
- [ ] Chips
- [ ] Crackers
- [ ] Pre-ground coffee

Fresh Ingredients

- [ ] Kale
- [ ] Spinach
- [ ] Potatoes
- [ ] Carrots
- [ ] Celery
- [ ] Tomatoes
- [ ] Ginger
- [ ] Onions
- [ ] Garlic
- [ ] Cilantro, dill, other herbs
- [ ] Avocados
- [ ] Lemons
- [ ] Limes
- [ ] Bananas
- [ ] Berries
- [ ] Other seasonal fruit, like pineapple, melon, mango

Dairy

- [ ] Eggs
- [ ] Milk
- [ ] Local cheeses
- [ ] Feta
- [ ] Butter
- [ ] Greek yogurt
- [ ] Buttermilk

Miscellaneous

- [ ] *The Sea Lover's Cookbook*
- [ ] Sweet spice mix (see page 20)
- [ ] Savory spice mix (see page 20)
- [ ] Water (still and sparkling)
- [ ] Tequila
- [ ] Wine
- [ ] Toilet paper
- [ ] Paper towels
- [ ] Dr. Bronner's soap
- [ ] Cheese grater
- [ ] Chef's knife

Farmers' Markets

Wherever your adventure begins, look for the local farmers' market—most places have one. I like to do a bit of research online before my trips to find the markets that will be near me at each destination. You can also ask a local, as they usually know the spots. Go to the market with reinforcements because you will need more than two hands to gather what you need, especially if you are cooking for multiple people. (Hot tip: Your docking office might have carts you can borrow, which is very helpful for transporting heavier items such as water, wine, etc.) I like to travel with a few tote bags to bring on shopping trips and a folding cooler bag if I can fit it in my luggage. The same strategy applies for when you are on vacation and staying in a home too.

I love exploring farmers' markets all over the world; they tell you so much about the local culture and the community. For example, when I traveled to Thailand, we went provisioning in a farmers' market in Phuket that was partially indoors. It was so cool to see how locals have their lunch! The fried rice was wrapped in white paper, and the curry came in an individual clear plastic bag. The curry paste was in humongous bowls that you could scoop yourself. Every place in the world has its story to tell, and being observant is such an amazing way to learn about other cultures and ways of living.

These markets also present a wonderful opportunity to explore and discover products and ingredients that you may not find at home. Observe what the locals are buying, as they know what tastes the best. Mingle with the community and stroll with a sense of curiosity. Keep an eye out for produce you're already familiar with, but look for the less familiar stuff too, and ask the vendors (if you share a common language) for tips on choosing the best item and preparing it to its greatest advantage. (A lot of places in the world study English as their second language, but it is nice to not assume right away. I like to write, "Do you speak English?" in the native tongue in a notepad or on my provisions list.)

SOME OF MY FAVORITE

port-of-call markets

Kallidromiou Farmers' Market
Athens, Greece
Make sure to buy fresh Greek yogurt from the cheese stand, and local honey.

Green Market
Split, Croatia
You can't miss the local fishermen with their latest catch.

The Sunday Market
Canggu, Bali
You can purchase the best fruits here, including one of my favorites, mangosteen!

The Farmers' Market
Phuket, Thailand
You'll find the tastiest curry paste and really affordable vanilla pods!

For example, when we were sailing in Thailand by the island of Ko Yao Noi, a fisherman came to our sailboat to sell us his catch of the day—big langoustines! He showed me how to clean the langoustine. I asked him how to cook it, and he understood my question well enough. He told me to simply marinate it in lime, salt, and pepper and cook it in a pan for 5 minutes with olive oil. I followed his suggestion exactly, and the dish turned out amazing—everyone on the boat loved it. So simple, yet so tasty. I suppose that's the beauty of fresh-out-of-the-ocean seafood. ∎

Water Appreciation

Let's honor the water and its ability to nurture us both physically and emotionally. The ocean makes up about three-quarters of our earth's surface. I love thinking about how the human body is made up of three-quarters water too. I don't believe this is a coincidence. Humans are a product of nature and we are all interconnected. It is so important that we value and protect the oceans and world around us. The sea is healing; it can cleanse your mind and invigorate your heart. Whenever you can, spend a few quiet moments by the water, close your eyes, listen to the lulling sound of the waves, and give thanks to the sea.

Part One

Mornings by the Water

This icy coffee beverage is fit for a sun-kissed vacation. Pair it with a slice of toasted Fig and Oat Bread (page 51) slathered in butter for breakfast. Or sip it after a little afternoon siesta for a delicious pick-me-up.

Coconut Cream Shaken Coffee

4 cups [945 ml] cold coffee

1 cup [240 ml] coconut cream

2 Tbsp maple syrup

½ cup [60 g] cocoa nibs

Big pinch of cinnamon

Ice, to serve

Makes 3 servings • In a large mason jar, combine the coffee, coconut cream, maple syrup, cocoa nibs, and cinnamon. Fit the lid on tightly and shake vigorously until the mixture is well combined and frothy, 20 to 30 seconds. Fill three tumbler glasses with ice and pour the shaken coffee over the top.

I love starting a beach day early, with a warm mug of this sweet and spicy turmeric latte. Most often, I make this with coconut milk, which is delicious, but you can use whatever type of milk you prefer. I'll sip on this latte as I make the Frittata with Greens and Crispy Potatoes (page 55) and wait for everyone else to wake up.

Warm Turmeric Latte

1 cup [240 ml] milk of choice

1 Tbsp honey

1 to 3 Tbsp
sweet spice mix (page 20)

Makes 1 serving • In a small saucepan over medium-low heat, warm the milk. Take the saucepan off the heat before the milk boils. Pour the warm milk into a mug. Add the honey and 1 Tbsp of the sweet spice mix, stirring to combine. Taste and add more spice mixture to your liking.

I make a version of this almost every day. My baby likes her milk warm in the morning, and so do I. My Ayurvedic doctor actually gave me the idea for this soothing recipe, as warm milk with dates in the morning is a really good way to support hormonal balance. Enjoy this by the ocean for the perfect start to a vacation.

"A Drink and Toast"

2 cups [480 ml] whole milk, or dairy-free milk of choice

6 dates, pitted (see Note)

4 green cardamom pods

1 cinnamon stick

½ vanilla bean or ¼ tsp vanilla extract

Pinch of kosher salt

2 slices good bread

¼ cup [55 g] salted butter, at room temperature

Flaky sea salt

Makes 2 servings • In a medium pot over low heat, warm the milk with the dates, cardamom, cinnamon, vanilla, and kosher salt. Bring to a simmer and keep over very low heat for about 30 minutes, breaking up the dates a bit with a wooden spoon. Do not let the mixture boil.

When the dates are soft and the milk is fragrant, strain the milk into mugs. Reserve the dates and discard the spices and vanilla bean, if using.

Toast the bread, spread with the butter, and top with the softened dates. Sprinkle a bit of flaky salt over the toast and serve alongside the spiced milk.

Note. Medjool dates work best here, but any type of date will do.

Most tropical fruits pair beautifully with lime juice. Just cut up any fruit you find at your local market during your travels, whether it be mango, papaya, or pineapple, and squeeze a lime over it to naturally bring out the juice of the fruit with a punchy and refreshing aftertaste. This recipe could not be simpler, yet it is so refreshing and delicious.

Fruit Salad with Lime and Honey

1½ to 2 lb [680 to 910 g] mixed fruit, such as pineapple, honeydew, mango, papaya, apple, or blueberries

Juice and zest of 2 limes

1 Tbsp honey

Small handful of mint leaves

Flaky sea salt

Makes 4 servings • Arrange the fruit on a beautiful platter or in a wide bowl in a fairly even layer. In a small jar or bowl, mix together the lime juice and honey, shaking or stirring vigorously to help the honey dissolve. Pour the mixture over the fruit, then sprinkle the lime zest over the top. Tear or thinly slice the mint leaves and scatter those over the top. Sprinkle with flaky salt and serve immediately.

Chia only needs about an hour to set into a pudding, so make this before your morning swim or beach walk. You can also make it the night before and store it in the fridge. Be aware that if you let it sit out too long in a warm climate, it turns somewhat quickly, so keep it in a cool place. Top it with your favorite fresh fruits, like berries or mangoes, or fruit compote.

Chia Pudding

½ cup [90 g] chia seeds

¼ tsp kosher salt

¼ tsp ground ginger

¼ tsp nutmeg, grated

One 13½ oz [400 ml] can light coconut milk (see Note)

1 Tbsp maple syrup

Fruit compote or jam, for serving

Makes 4 to 6 servings • In a medium bowl with a tight-fitting lid, mix together the chia seeds, salt, ginger, and nutmeg. Add the coconut milk and maple syrup and stir well. Refrigerate for at least 6 hours and preferably overnight.

To serve, put a spoonful or two of compote or jam in the bottom of a small jar or bowl. Scoop a portion of the chia pudding over the top, mix to incorporate, and enjoy.

Note. You can use full-fat coconut milk, but make sure the can is shaken well. You may need to warm it a bit to integrate the solid cream with the liquid.

Maybe you thought the world didn't need another gluten-free pancake recipe, but this one is special because it uses yogurt in lieu of buttermilk. Most of us are more likely to have a tub of plain yogurt in the fridge than a bottle of buttermilk, and I wanted a pancake recipe that could be made on a whim. The pro move is to measure and combine the dry ingredients the night before so you'll have time to jump in the ocean before you start frying.

Cornmeal Pancakes

1½ cups [210 g] cornmeal

½ cup [60 g] oat flour

2 Tbsp granulated sugar

2 tsp baking powder

1½ tsp kosher salt

1 tsp baking soda

2 cups [480 g] full-fat yogurt

2 large eggs

2 Tbsp unsalted butter, melted

Coconut or grapeseed oil, for greasing the pan

Maple syrup, for serving

Makes 8 pancakes • In a large bowl, mix together the cornmeal, oat flour, sugar, baking powder, salt, and baking soda and set aside. In a medium bowl, whisk together the yogurt and eggs. Pour the yogurt mixture and melted butter into the dry mixture, folding gently until just combined—a few lumps are okay. If you have time, let the batter rest for 15 minutes before frying the pancakes.

Heat a large nonstick or cast-iron skillet over medium heat and add about 1 Tbsp of oil. Add about ⅓ cup [60 g] of batter to the pan. Add a second pancake if two can fit comfortably on your skillet without touching. When you notice bubbles forming on the surface of the batter, flip the pancake—if that first side is very brown, lower the heat a bit. If it's pale, raise the heat. Repeat with the remaining batter, keeping the finished pancakes warm with tented foil or in a warming drawer, if you have one. Drizzle with maple syrup and serve immediately.

Homemade granola can seem intimidating, but with the right ratios of grains, nuts, oil, and a natural sweetener (and plenty of salt!) you can easily make a version that exactly suits your tastes. I like the combination of earthy buckwheat and warming ginger for its grounding and digestion-soothing effects, but you can easily swap out the buckwheat hulls for more oats if you can't find them.

This granola is a good candidate to make before your trip. It's easy to pack and lasts a long time. Be warned: Your guests will start to request your signature granola on future vacations! This is delicious served with yogurt and fruit.

Buckwheat Ginger Granola

3 cups [300 g] old-fashioned oats

1 cup [180 g] buckwheat groats

¾ cup [90 g] pecans, roughly chopped

¼ cup [35 g] sunflower seeds

¼ cup [35 g] sesame seeds

¼ cup [40 g] ground flax seeds

2 Tbsp chia seeds

½ cup [120 ml] maple syrup

½ cup [120 ml] olive oil

1 egg white

1 Tbsp plus 1 tsp ground ginger

1½ tsp kosher salt

½ tsp cinnamon

Makes 2 qt [760 g] • Preheat the oven to 325°F [165°C]. In a large bowl, mix together the oats, buckwheat, pecans, and all the seeds. In a medium bowl, whisk together the maple syrup, olive oil, egg white, ginger, salt, and cinnamon until smooth. Pour the wet mixture into the dry mixture and stir well until the oats are completely coated.

Line a large rimmed baking sheet with parchment paper or a silicone baking mat and spread the granola mixture evenly across the pan. Bake for 20 minutes, rotate the sheet, and stir, bringing the browning bits on the edges toward the center of the sheet and the center bits toward the outside. Bake for 18 to 20 minutes more, or until fragrant and golden. Do not stir until completely cooled. Store in an airtight container for up to 3 weeks.

Not all beach trips are warm. Many of my vacation days by the sea are in my home in mid-coast Maine, and I love to walk down to the water early in the morning. Often, it's chilly and foggy, so a hot breakfast is really satisfying.

I find this oatmeal to be so nurturing. Turmeric has many health benefits, like helping with inflammation in the body and easing digestion. If you're taking this on a boat trip, mix the oats with the spices before you leave and take it on board in a Ziploc bag.

Turmeric Oatmeal

2 cups [200 g] old-fashioned oats (not quick cooking)

4 Tbsp sweet spice mix (page 20)

One 13½ oz [400 ml] can full-fat coconut milk

Maple syrup or honey, to taste

Salt, to taste

Ghee, grass-fed butter, olive oil, or coconut butter, for serving

Toasted coconut flakes, for serving (optional)

Dried or fresh fruit, such as chopped dates, raisins, or fresh blueberries, for serving (optional)

Makes 4 servings • In a medium pot over medium heat, add the oats and spice mix. Stir frequently until the oats smell toasted and the spices are fragrant. Add the coconut milk and 2¼ cups [540 ml] of water, bring to a boil, then lower the heat and simmer. Cook over low heat, stirring occasionally, until the oats are tender and the liquid is absorbed, 8 to 10 minutes. Add the maple syrup to taste and salt to taste, and top with a spoonful of ghee, toasted coconut flakes, if using, and fruit, if using. Serve immediately.

These breakfast bars are easy to wrap and bring on the go, and they make for a great breakfast treat or a midday snack. I like to make them in the summer in Maine with just-picked wild blueberries, wrap them in wax paper, and bring them to my favorite swimming spot, a freshwater quarry near our house. If you're enjoying these bars in the afternoon, serve with a scoop of ice cream on top.

Blueberry Granola Breakfast Bars

Olive oil, for greasing the pan

1 cup [95 g] Buckwheat Ginger Granola (page 44)

1 cup [20 g] puffed brown rice cereal

½ cup [170 g] almond butter

½ cup [70 g] almonds, chopped

½ cup [70 g] dried blueberries

¼ cup [60 ml] maple syrup

½ tsp kosher salt

Makes 12 bars • Line an 8 in [20 cm] square baking pan with parchment paper. (Use a bit of olive oil to help the parchment stick to the pan.) Mix all of the ingredients together in a large bowl and press into the pan. Spread the mixture very evenly, then cover with another piece of parchment paper. Use a flat-bottomed cup or jar to press down and smooth out the mixture. Let sit overnight, unrefrigerated, so the flavors meld and come together.

Invert the pan onto a cutting board and slice into twelve bars. Store the bars in a tin box or Ziploc bag in the shade for up to 3 days.

When *traveling* with multiple people, it's really important to try and get *everyone involved* in cooking. Not only does it take the pressure off of you, but it also gives other people something productive to do, which is usually *welcome* and makes for a *more fun* experience all around. Delegate chores and allow autonomy. Nobody likes a controlling person in the kitchen. Allow for things to not go your way, and stay *open-minded* for a more *positive experience.*

This recipe was inspired by flourless Scandinavian seed and nut breads, which are nutrient dense and hold up really well—great qualities for boat fare. This version uses oats, almonds, and pumpkin seeds, with figs and a touch of maple syrup for sweetness. It's delicious with a smear of cultured butter (don't forget the flaky salt) and a cup of strong coffee, or with a slice of sharp cheddar and an aperitif.

Fig and Oat Bread

¼ cup [60 ml] olive oil, plus more for greasing the pan

4 eggs

1 Tbsp maple syrup

1 tsp kosher salt

2½ cups [250 g] old-fashioned oats

½ cup [70 g] almonds

½ cup [70 g] packed dried figs

½ cup [70 g] pumpkin seeds

Makes 1 loaf • Preheat the oven to 350°F [180°C]. Oil an 8½ by 4½ in [21.5 by 11 cm] loaf pan with olive oil and set aside.

In a large bowl, whisk together the olive oil, eggs, maple syrup, and salt. Place the oats and almonds in a food processor and process on high speed for about 30 seconds, or until the oats are partially ground and the almonds are roughly chopped. Add the mixture to the bowl with the eggs. Place the figs in the food processor and process on high speed until they're chopped—you may need to pulse the food processor if the figs start to become pasty. You want them in pea-size pieces. Add the figs and pumpkin seeds to the egg-oat mixture and stir well. Scrape the batter into the prepared pan and bake for 1 hour, rotating the pan after 30 minutes. The oats should be golden brown and the bread quite firm.

Let cool completely, remove the loaf from the pan, then slice thinly and serve. The bread will keep, wrapped, on the counter for about 1 week.

This warm broth can be sipped at any time of day, but I love occasionally replacing my morning coffee with a cup of this. It's simple but nourishing, and provides me with what I need to face whatever's on the agenda. For a richer broth, opt for the vegetable broth instead of the water. You can use unsalted ghee, but make sure to add a pinch of flaky salt to boost the flavor.

Ginger Broth with Ghee

4 in [10 cm] piece of ginger, roughly chopped

1 bay leaf

6 in [15 cm] piece of dried kombu

¼ tsp ground turmeric

6 cups [1.4 L] water or vegetable broth

Juice of 1 lemon

Kosher salt

Freshly ground black pepper

Salted ghee, for serving

Makes 4 servings • In a medium pot over medium-low heat, simmer the ginger, bay leaf, kombu, turmeric, and water for 30 minutes. Strain, add the lemon juice, and season with salt and pepper. Serve in a mug with a spoonful of salted ghee.

In Asian cultures, soup is a common breakfast item for many fishermen. This recipe is inspired by my travels in Thailand, where the fish markets right by the water provide a bounty of ingredients. I love making this on chillier mornings when the wind whips the sea and I need to feel fortified. This soup takes about 20 minutes to come together, but it is packed with nutrients and will warm and sustain you all morning. Reheat leftovers the next morning...the flavors keep getting better and better as they marinate!

Turmeric Miso Breakfast Soup

4 cups [945 ml] vegetable stock

½ tsp ground turmeric

1 in [2.5 cm] piece of ginger, peeled and cut into matchsticks

Small handful of dried wakame seaweed

2 small carrots, thinly sliced

½ daikon radish, thinly sliced

Small handful of any mushroom variety, thinly sliced if large

1 small red chile, thinly sliced (optional)

2 Tbsp miso paste

2 eggs, soft-boiled, peeled, and halved

Pinch of red pepper flakes

Makes 4 servings • In a medium saucepan over medium-high heat, bring the stock to a simmer. Add the turmeric and ginger and let simmer for 3 minutes.

Meanwhile, in a small bowl, cover the dried seaweed with water to rehydrate it.

Add the rehydrated seaweed, carrots, daikon radish, mushrooms, and chile, if using, to the broth and simmer for 3 minutes.

Turn off the heat and ladle a small amount of the broth into a small bowl. Using a fork, stir in the miso paste. Once the miso has dissolved and the mixture is smooth, add it back into the saucepan of soup. Ladle out each portion of soup, top with half an egg and red pepper flakes, and serve.

This is a perfect savory breakfast meal that transforms into a delicious lunch served with a green salad on the side—that is, if there's anything left. Don't be shy when it comes to cooking the potatoes, as the crispy-crunch you achieve by browning them is extremely satisfying.

Frittata with Greens and Crispy Potatoes

¼ cup [60 ml] olive oil

1 yellow onion, thinly sliced

1 bunch kale, stemmed and finely chopped

Kosher salt

Freshly ground black pepper

Juice of ½ lemon

8 eggs

½ cup [120 g] full-fat yogurt

4 oz [115 g] feta, crumbled

1 lb [455 g] potatoes, any variety, peeled and thinly sliced

Makes 8 servings • Preheat the oven to 325°F [165°C] (do not use the convection setting, if you have one). Heat a 10 in [25 cm] cast-iron skillet over medium heat and add 2 Tbsp of the olive oil. Add the onion and sauté, stirring often, for about 10 minutes, or until soft and starting to caramelize. Add the kale and season with salt and pepper. Sauté for about 5 minutes until the kale is tender, adding a splash of water if the pan seems dry. Add the lemon juice, mix well, and transfer the mixture to a medium bowl to cool.

Meanwhile, in a large bowl, whisk the eggs with the yogurt. Add the feta and season with plenty of salt and pepper. Set aside.

Add the remaining 2 Tbsp of olive oil to the same skillet, increase the heat to medium-high, and add the potatoes. Season well with salt and pepper and cook, stirring often with a flexible spatula, until the potatoes are cooked through and starting to brown. If the browning happens too quickly, turn the heat down to medium. Moving the potatoes around the skillet can be a bit awkward, so don't worry if some of the potatoes break.

When the potatoes are done, arrange them in an even layer in the skillet and remove from the heat. Add the kale-onion mixture to the eggs, stir well, and pour the whole thing into the skillet over the potatoes. Shake the pan a bit to distribute the eggs evenly and transfer to the oven. Bake for about 30 minutes, checking and rotating the pan after 15 minutes. The frittata is done when the top is just set—if it feels like the center is set (not jiggly) but the top is still wet, you can pop it under the broiler for a minute or two.

Remove the skillet from the oven, let cool, and invert the frittata onto a plate. Feel free to display inverted or not—the potatoes can be really beautiful! Serve immediately.

These mini frittatas, which we've playfully dubbed *frittatettas*, are muffin-size and perfect for on-the-go adventures. I sometimes travel with my silicone muffin cups, as they take up barely any space in a suitcase or on a boat and are very useful for making muffins, these frittatettas, and more.

Frittatettas

1 Tbsp olive oil, plus more for the muffin cups

1 onion, diced

6 garlic cloves, smashed

½ tsp red pepper flakes (optional)

2 cups [40 g] baby spinach

Kosher salt

Freshly ground black pepper

8 eggs

½ cup [120 g] full-fat ricotta

½ cup [40 g] grated mozzarella or fontina, plus twelve ½ in [13 mm] cubes

½ cup [20 g] chopped parsley

12 slices prosciutto (about 4 oz [115 g]), optional

Makes 12 frittatettas • Preheat the oven to 300°F [150°C]. In a large skillet over medium heat, heat the olive oil. Add the onion, garlic, and red pepper flakes, if using, and cook for 10 minutes, or until the onion is soft and the garlic is golden. Add the spinach, season with salt and pepper, and cook until the spinach wilts, about 3 minutes. Remove from the heat and set aside.

In a large bowl, whisk the eggs with the ricotta and season with salt and pepper. Add the grated mozzarella, parsley, and spinach-onion mixture. If you're using prosciutto, carefully line each cup of a nonstick 12-cup muffin tin (not jumbo!) with a single piece of prosciutto—it's okay if it folds over the top of the cup a bit, you just want to make sure there are no spots left uncovered. If you're not using prosciutto, grease the muffin cups with olive oil, wiping with a paper towel for even coverage.

Divide the egg mixture evenly among the cups and top each with a mozzarella cube. Place the muffin tin in the oven and bake for about 20 minutes, turning the tin once halfway through. The frittatettas are done when they're puffed up and firm to the touch. Let cool for at least 10 minutes in the muffin tin—you may wish to use a flexible offset spatula or butter knife, depending on the material of your tin, to help coax them out of the cups. Frittatettas will keep for up to 3 days tightly wrapped in the refrigerator. Bring to room temperature or warm in the oven to serve.

What's better than fresh pasta? Crispy pasta the next day! This recipe couldn't be any easier. You can use any shape of pasta you want here—penne, spaghetti, orecchiette—whatever you have left over in your fridge. Don't be shy with the amount of herbs you put on this one. (Here's an easy and mess-free trick for cutting herbs: Place a mix of herbs in an empty water glass, and cut the herbs inside the glass with scissors.)

Crispy Pasta with Fried Eggs

¼ cup [60 ml] plus 2 Tbsp olive oil

⅓ cup [10 g] freshly grated Parmesan

About 4 cups [800 g] leftover pasta

2 eggs

Flaky sea salt

Freshly ground black pepper

½ cup [20 g] chopped tender herbs, such as parsley, mint, or dill

Makes 2 servings • In a medium nonstick or cast-iron skillet over medium-high heat, warm ¼ cup [60 ml] of the olive oil. Sprinkle the Parmesan evenly in the pan and spoon the pasta directly over the top, nestling it in so lots of pasta is making contact with the cheesy bottom of the pan. Cover and cook for 3 minutes, or until the pasta is warmed through. Uncover and cook for 3 more minutes to let some moisture evaporate.

Run a flexible spatula under the pasta to loosen it from the pan and divide it between two bowls, making sure the crispy, browned cheesy bits are on top.

Add the remaining 2 Tbsp of olive oil to the same pan and fry the eggs to your liking. Top each bowl with a fried egg, salt, pepper, and the herbs. Serve immediately.

Wake up, make coffee, jump in the ocean for a morning dip, make these biscuit sandwiches, and pull up the anchor to head to your next adventure spot! That is an ideal morning. This recipe calls for the Rye Vinegar Biscuits on page 66, but you can also use store-bought rolls in a pinch. I recommend making the biscuits a day or two before so that these sandwiches take less time to prep. If made ahead, the rye vinegar biscuits can be reheated at 250°F [120°C] for 5 minutes before you assemble the sandwich. Also note that the pickled onions need to be made at least one day in advance.

Captain's Breakfast Sandwich

6 eggs

Kosher salt

Freshly ground black pepper

2 Tbsp unsalted butter

6 slices (3 oz [85 g]) cheddar cheese

4 Rye Vinegar Biscuits (page 66)

½ cup [10 g] parsley leaves and tender stems

¼ cup [45 g] Overnight Pickled Onions (recipe follows)

Olive oil

Makes 4 servings • Crack 3 eggs into one small bowl and 3 into another small bowl. Season both bowls with salt and pepper and whisk very well.

In an 8 in [20 cm] nonstick skillet, warm 1 Tbsp of the butter over medium-low heat. Pour in one bowl of eggs and stir slowly and constantly for 1 minute. Let the eggs sit undisturbed for another minute, then begin to lift up the cooked edges with a heatproof spatula and gently tip the pan to let the uncooked egg flow underneath. When the egg is mostly cooked, place three slices of cheese on half of the omelet, then fold the omelet in half to cover the cheese. Cook for 1 minute more, then transfer the omelet to a cutting board. Let it rest so the cheese melts and the egg cooks through, then cut in half. Meanwhile, repeat with the remaining butter, eggs, and cheese.

Split the biscuits open and place an omelet portion on the bottom half of each biscuit. Top with the parsley and pickled onions, drizzle with olive oil, and sprinkle with salt and pepper. Place the other halves of the biscuits on top and serve.

Overnight Pickled Onions

**1 medium red onion,
thinly sliced**

**1 cup [240 ml] rice vinegar
or white vinegar**

1 Tbsp kosher salt

1 Tbsp granulated sugar

Makes 2 cups [360 g] • Place the onion, vinegar, salt, and sugar in a mason jar. Seal the lid and shake well. Store in the refrigerator overnight to quick-pickle the onions. Strain the onions before using. Store, sealed, in a cool, dry place for up to 1 week.

Whoever invented the burrito is a genius. Not only is it filling and packed with flavor, but it doesn't need to be plated, which is great when you reside in small quarters! Take this burrito and go sit on a dock or the stern to enjoy the ocean views.

Burrito Mucho

Potatoes

1 medium or 2 small sweet potatoes (about 1 lb [455 g]), peeled and cut into slabs

2 Tbsp neutral oil, such as grapeseed

Kosher salt

Freshly ground black pepper

Beans

1 Tbsp neutral oil, such as grapeseed

½ small onion, diced (about ½ cup [70 g])

½ tsp chili powder

½ tsp ground cumin

1½ cups [240 g] cooked beans, such as pinto, or one 15 oz [425 g] can pinto beans, drained

1 garlic clove, grated

Kosher salt

Juice of 1 lime, or to taste

Cilantro Crema

½ cup [10 g] cilantro leaves and tender stems

1 jalapeño, halved (seeded if you like)

1 garlic clove

Zest and juice of 1 lime (see Note)

½ cup [120 g] full-fat yogurt or sour cream

Kosher salt

Scrambled Eggs

6 eggs

Kosher salt

Freshly ground black pepper

1 Tbsp unsalted butter

½ tsp ground cumin (optional)

Assembly

4 burrito-size tortillas

4 oz [115 g] pepper Jack cheese, shredded

Overnight Pickled Onions (page 61) or store-bought pickled onion or jalapeño (optional)

Makes 4 burritos • To make the potatoes: Preheat the oven to 400°F [200°C]. Toss the sweet potato slabs in the oil, salt, and pepper on a large rimmed baking sheet. Roast in the oven until tender and golden, about 20 minutes. Remove from the oven, then cover the sweet potatoes with a sheet of parchment paper. It doesn't need to fit perfectly, but it keeps the heat in and steams the potatoes a bit, making them soft and not so crispy. con't »

To make the beans: In a medium pot over medium heat, heat the oil. Add the onion, season with salt and pepper, and sauté until soft, about 10 minutes. Add the chili powder and cumin and let the spices bloom for a minute. Add the beans, garlic, and a splash of water or bean cooking liquid. Mix well, smashing the beans with a wooden spoon. Add a small amount of water or turn the heat down if it gets very thick and pasty. Season with salt and the lime juice to taste, then set aside.

To make the cilantro crema: Chop the cilantro, jalapeño, garlic, and lime zest together on a cutting board until finely minced and integrated. Put in a medium bowl along with the yogurt and lime juice. Season the crema with salt and set aside.

To make the eggs: Whisk the eggs in a medium bowl and season with salt and pepper. Add 1 to 2 Tbsp of water. In a large ovenproof skillet over medium heat, heat the butter, then add the cumin, if using. When the cumin starts to sputter, add the eggs and scramble quickly, stirring the whole time.

To assemble the burritos: On a clean, flat surface, lay out the tortillas. Spread the beans evenly down the centers—you may have a bit extra. Sprinkle the cheese evenly over the beans. Spoon the scrambled eggs over the cheese. Lay a few sweet potato slabs over the eggs, drizzle with cilantro crema, and top with pickled onion, if using. Roll up the burritos. You can wrap the burritos in parchment paper or aluminum foil to make them more portable.

Note. Zest your lime before juicing it. It's much easier to zest a whole lime than a halved one. You can make these burritos up to 1 day ahead of time: Store them, wrapped, in the refrigerator, and then reheat in a 300°F [150°C] oven until they're warmed through, 25 to 30 minutes.

The splash of vinegar in this recipe adds extra acid to the buttermilk, which reacts with the baking soda, lightening and lifting the coarse rye flour. This creates a light, flaky biscuit with the nutty flavor and complex mouthfeel of whole grains. Make the butter mixture ahead of time and store it in a quart container or Ziploc bag in the freezer. All you'll have to do on the boat is find something that can approximate a rolling pin (one of last night's wine bottles?) and crank up your oven.

Rye Vinegar Biscuits

1 cup [110 g] dark rye flour

2 cups [280 g] all-purpose flour, plus more for dusting

2 Tbsp granulated sugar

1 Tbsp kosher salt

1 Tbsp baking powder

¼ tsp baking soda

¾ cup [170 g] cold unsalted butter

1¼ cups [300 ml] buttermilk

1 egg

1 tsp apple cider vinegar

Flaky sea salt

Makes 8 biscuits • Preheat the oven to 425°F [220°C] if you're baking right away, and line a baking sheet with parchment paper.

In a large bowl, mix together the flours, sugar, salt, baking powder, and baking soda. Working quickly, grate the butter into the dry ingredients using the large holes of a box grater. Toss the mixture with your hands until the butter is distributed throughout. (This step can be done up to 1 week ahead, stored in the refrigerator, or kept indefinitely in the freezer.)

When you're ready to bake, in a mason jar or small bowl, shake or mix together the buttermilk, egg, and vinegar. Reserve about ¼ cup [60 ml] and pour the remaining liquid into the bowl with the dry ingredients. Stir gently with a spoon or your fingers until the liquid is mostly incorporated but plenty of dry spots remain.

Transfer the dough to a clean work surface and gently bring everything together, pressing and patting with your hands to make a cohesive ball. Pat it into a rectangle, then fold in half short end to short end. Repeat this a few times. Lightly flour the work surface, then roll (with a rolling pin or a wine bottle) into a rectangle about 12 by 6 in [30.5 by 15 cm].

Flip the dough over so the smooth surface is now facing up. Cut the dough in half lengthwise, then crosswise three times to make eight square biscuits. Flip the biscuits over again, so the smooth side is once again facing up. This flip trick gives you beautiful defined edges. (If you'd like the prettiest biscuits possible, trim the exterior edges of the rectangle before cutting into portions, then make a round biscuit shape with the scraps of dough.)

Space the biscuits evenly on the prepared baking sheet, brush lightly with the reserved buttermilk mixture, sprinkle with flaky salt, and place on the top rack in the oven. Bake for 10 minutes, rotate the pan, and then bake 6 to 8 minutes more, until the tops are golden brown and a biscuit easily splits apart. Serve right away, or let cool and store for up to 1 day in a tightly sealed container.

Sustainable Boating Practices

I try to be as eco-conscious as possible when traveling, especially on the water. It is almost impossible to take sailing trips and not pollute, but we can try to be as aware as possible to minimize our carbon footprint and waste. Here are easy ways to preserve water and use sustainable practices while boating.

- All dishes can be pre-cleaned with seawater and then rinsed with fresh water. I make a soapy bowl using a non-toxic soap (like Dr. Bronner's), take it to the stern along with my dirty dishes, and do a wash and rinse in the ocean. When all the dishes are done, I do a final quick rinse with the fresh water from the boat.

- When I'm on a boat trip, my showers consist of diving into the ocean and doing a quick rinse with fresh water from the stern. This not only helps preserve the water tank but also allows for a great hair day every day.

- When I was cooking on boats more regularly, I used to keep a bowl nearby to collect anything that I could throw in the ocean, like fish bones, shells, and vegetable scraps—essentially anything that would disintegrate quickly and easily, and anything that a fish could safely eat. Doing so helps minimize your trash—think of it as composting at sea.

- Also consider the beauty products that you use. When you splash around in the ocean or take a shower on the stern of the boat, the soap and any products on your skin flow into the sea. There are so many cool beauty brands out there now that are environmentally friendly (Dr. Bronner's, again!). Try to use eco-friendly body products—and maybe skip your makeup altogether.

Light Meals on Deck

This is my go-to salad when I'm short on time.
Easy prep, crunchy and refreshing, and tons of flavor!

Green Salad

1 garlic clove, grated

Juice of 1 lemon,
plus more as needed

Kosher salt

½ medium head romaine
lettuce, torn (about 6 oz [170 g])

4 celery stalks,
thinly sliced on a bias

½ medium English cucumber,
sliced into ½ in [13 mm] chunks
(about 6 oz [170 g])

1 avocado, cubed

1 cup [20 g] mixed tender herbs,
finely chopped

2 Tbsp olive oil

Freshly ground black pepper

4 oz [115 g] good-quality
cheddar cheese, crumbled
into irregular pieces

Makes 4 servings • In a large bowl, add the garlic, lemon juice, and a big pinch of kosher salt. Add the lettuce, celery, cucumber, avocado, and herbs to the bowl and toss well. Add the olive oil and pepper and toss again. Taste for seasoning and add more salt or lemon juice as needed. Crumble the cheddar into the salad, toss gently, and serve.

Having a jar of great sauce on hand will serve you well on vacation, because it means delicious, effortless meals and snacks are always within reach. This recipe makes about twice the peanut sauce you'll need for this flavor-packed salad, so you can look forward to dipping Fresh Vietnamese-Style Spring Rolls (page 128) in the leftover sauce, tossing it with noodles, or serving it with fried eggs, hot sauce, and a giant tangle of cilantro.

Crunchy Cabbage Salad with Peanut Sauce

Peanut Sauce

3 garlic cloves, grated

1 in [2.5 cm] piece of ginger, grated

2 Tbsp rice vinegar

2 Tbsp lime juice

¾ cup [260 g] creamy peanut butter

¼ cup [60 ml] maple syrup

¼ cup [60 ml] tamari or shoyu (use low-sodium if you're also using fish sauce)

2 Tbsp toasted sesame oil

½ tsp fish sauce (optional)

Salad

½ red onion, thinly sliced

¼ cup [60 ml] rice vinegar

Kosher salt

½ medium cabbage (about 1 lb [455 g]), thinly sliced

2 or 3 medium carrots, shredded

½ cup [10 g] mixed herbs, such as mint, cilantro, Thai basil, or shiso

Freshly ground black pepper

¼ cup [35 g] roasted salted peanuts, chopped

Lime wedges, for garnish

Makes 4 servings • **To make the peanut sauce:** In a large bowl, mix together the garlic, ginger, vinegar, and lime juice. Let sit for 5 minutes, then add the peanut butter, maple syrup, tamari, sesame oil, and fish sauce, if using. Add ¼ cup [60 ml] of water and whisk together well, adding 1 Tbsp or so more water as needed for a thick but smooth and pourable sauce (it will thicken as it sits). Set aside.

To make the salad: In a large bowl, mix the onion with the vinegar and a big pinch of salt. Let sit for about 5 minutes, toss well, then add the cabbage, carrot, and half the herbs. Season with salt and pepper and toss well. To serve, spread about half of the peanut sauce on a wide platter or shallow serving bowl. (Reserve the remaining sauce for another use.) Pile the cabbage mixture over the peanut sauce, letting some sauce show through around the edges. Scatter the remaining herbs over the cabbage, followed by the peanuts. Garnish with lime wedges and serve.

The addition of crispy chickpeas makes this salad filling and fun to eat. I love the colors from the chicory leaves too. I like to serve this hearty salad with a cold bottle of Greek white wine like Assyrtiko, or an Australian Grüner.

Hearty Salad

Crispy Chickpeas

¼ cup [60 ml] neutral oil, such as grapeseed

1 tsp smoked paprika

½ tsp ground cumin

One 15 oz [425 g] can chickpeas, drained and patted dry

Kosher salt

Freshly ground black pepper

Dressing

1 medium shallot, thinly sliced

2 Tbsp lime juice (from 1 lime)

Kosher salt

Freshly ground black pepper

2 Tbsp olive oil

1 Tbsp maple syrup

Salad

1 head radicchio or other chicory (about 4 cups [300 g]), torn

½ cup [70 g] black olives, pitted and roughly chopped

¼ cup [35 g] toasted pumpkin seeds

3 oz [85 g] feta, crumbled

Makes 4 servings • To make the crispy chickpeas: In a medium skillet over medium-high heat, warm the oil. Add the paprika and cumin and let them bloom for about 30 seconds. Add the chickpeas, stir well to coat, season with salt and pepper, and fry for 8 to 10 minutes, or until the chickpeas are starting to crisp. Use a slotted spoon to scoop them out of the pan and place on a paper towel–lined plate; set aside.

To make the dressing: In a large bowl, add the shallot, lime juice, and a big pinch of salt. Let sit for 5 minutes. Add a few grinds of pepper, the olive oil, and maple syrup and swirl the bowl to mix. Taste for seasoning and add salt as needed.

To make the salad: To the bowl with dressing, add the radicchio, olives, pumpkin seeds, and feta and toss well. Add the crispy chickpeas and toss gently. Serve immediately.

This recipe is one of my daughter's favorites. The sweet grilled corn with the bright lime juice and cilantro is a winning combination. Serve this salad alongside Fish Tacos (page 154) for dinner. Keep any leftovers for tomorrow's lunch—this salad is just as good served cold.

Grilled Corn Salad

2 garlic cloves

½ tsp smoked paprika

Juice of 3 limes, plus more as needed

Kosher salt

Freshly ground black pepper

6 ears of corn, shucked

3 Tbsp neutral oil, such as grapeseed

4 scallions

½ cup [10 g] cilantro, roughly chopped

¼ cup [35 g] toasted pumpkin seeds, chopped

¼ cup [8 g] grated Parmesan

Makes 4 servings • Prepare a grill for high heat.

Grate the garlic into a large bowl, add the paprika and lime juice, and season with salt and pepper. Let sit while you grill the corn. Rub the corn with 2 Tbsp of the oil and season it with salt and pepper. Grill the corn, turning occasionally, until very well charred, about 15 minutes.

Meanwhile, lightly coat the scallions with the remaining 1 Tbsp of oil and season with salt. Grill for 2 to 3 minutes per side, or until lightly charred. Let the corn and scallions cool.

When the corn comes off the grill, stand the cobs upright and slice the kernels off the cobs with a sharp knife. (Prepare yourself for a bit of a mess, and use the largest cutting board you can find!) Thinly slice the scallions. Add the corn, scallions, cilantro, pumpkin seeds, and Parmesan to the bowl with the garlic mixture and toss well. Season with more salt and lime juice as needed.

This is a pretty straightforward sandwich formula—good bread, something pickled, something green, something protein-dense, and something luxurious to bind it all together. Taking the time to make mayonnaise from scratch will turn an otherwise basic sandwich into something truly special. And tucking potato chips in at the last minute adds amazing crunch and gives it a deliciously low-brow vibe.

Five-Layer Sandwich

Mayonnaise

1 small garlic clove, grated or minced

1 large egg yolk, at room temperature

1 tsp lemon juice

1 tsp white vinegar

1 tsp Dijon mustard

1 tsp cold water

½ tsp kosher salt

½ cup [120 ml] neutral oil, such as grapeseed or avocado

¼ cup [60 ml] olive oil

Sandwiches

4 eggs

8 slices good-quality bread

1 avocado, sliced

Kosher salt

Freshly ground black pepper

2 cups [40 g] arugula

1 cup [160 g] Overnight Pickles (page 112)

1 bag of your favorite potato chips (salt-and-pepper kettle chips are great here)

Makes 4 sandwiches • **To make the mayonnaise:** In a medium bowl, whisk together the garlic, egg yolk, lemon juice, vinegar, mustard, water, and salt. In a cup with a spout, mix together the neutral oil and olive oil, then slowly drizzle it into the bowl, whisking vigorously (a drop or two at a time at first, and then in a thin stream after the mayonnaise begins to thicken). When all the oil has been added, set aside.

To make the sandwiches: Bring a medium pot of water to a boil. Lower the eggs in and boil for 8 minutes. Remove from the pot and let sit at room temperature until cool enough to handle, then peel and slice them.

Lightly toast the bread on a grill or under the broiler. Spread four slices with the mayonnaise and divide the avocado among the other slices, gently smashing it into the bread with a fork. Season the avocado with salt and pepper. Arrange the sliced eggs on the mayonnaise-covered bread and season with salt and pepper. Top the eggs with the arugula, pickles, and potato chips. Place the avocado-covered bread over the arugula to close the sandwiches. Serve immediately.

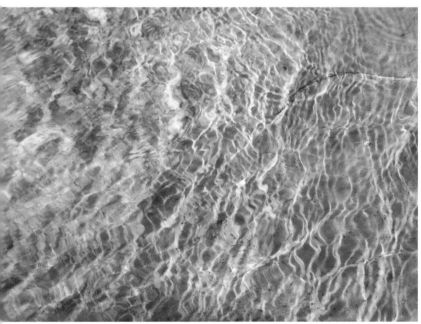

Swimming in *open water* doesn't have to be restricted to summertime. I have a friend who takes a dip in the ocean almost *every morning*, and she lives in Maine, where the water can be around 50°F [10°C]! Not for the faint of heart, but if you *feel courageous*, cold dips are *invigorating*, and some researchers believe they help decrease inflammation and manage moods. The *rush of endorphins*, when experienced as part of a healthy routine, has changed some people's overall *spirit*.

My husband and I are mostly vegetarians (I say *mostly* because I eat fish sometimes). This vegetarian banh mi offers Vietnamese flavors with a French flair. It's perfect for a beach day. I wrap the sandwiches in wax paper and tie them with a string or rubber band so the ingredients don't move around. Whether you are baking the tofu like the recipe asks for here or sautéing it in a pan for another dish, don't skip the pressing step. Getting as much moisture as possible out of the tofu before cooking it is key to making this ingredient shine.

Bok Choy Banh Mi

One 14 oz [400 g] package extra-firm tofu

2 Tbsp soy sauce

1 garlic clove, grated

1 in [2.5 cm] piece of ginger, grated

1 Tbsp granulated sugar

1 Tbsp cornstarch

½ tsp cinnamon

1 Tbsp neutral oil, such as grapeseed

Kosher salt

1 medium head bok choy or 4 baby bok choy

1 cup [240 g] mayonnaise

1 Tbsp sriracha

2 soft baguettes or loaves of French bread, halved crosswise, or 4 long rolls

1 cup [160 g] Overnight Pickles (page 112)

2 cups [40 g] mixed herbs, such as mint, basil, and cilantro

Makes 4 sandwiches • Preheat the oven to 350°F [180°C]. Drain the tofu and slice it into eight thin rectangles. Spread them out on a kitchen towel, cover with another towel, and then set a cookie sheet with a weight on top. Let sit for at least 15 minutes to press out the moisture.

In a medium bowl, mix together the soy sauce, garlic, ginger, sugar, cornstarch, cinnamon, and oil, whisking until smooth. Dip each tofu slice in the marinade and spread them out on a baking sheet lined with parchment paper; reserve the marinade. Bake the tofu for 45 minutes, rotating the pan and basting with marinade halfway through. The tofu will be dark in color and feel dry to the touch. Set aside to cool.

Meanwhile, prepare the bok choy. Bring a large pot of well-salted water to a boil. Blanch the bok choy for approximately 3 minutes, or until bright green and barely tender. Drain and finely chop. Set aside.

In a medium bowl, mix together the mayonnaise and sriracha.

To assemble the sandwiches, split the bread in half and lightly toast in the oven for 5 minutes. Spread the sriracha mayonnaise on both sides. Divide the bok choy among the bottom halves. Place two slices of tofu over the bok choy on each sandwich, then spread the pickles over the tofu. Top them with a generous pile of herbs, close the sandwiches, and serve.

The cumin in this egg salad is the secret weapon. It really makes it a bit different and more interesting than the old deli-counter staple. Overnight Pickles (page 112) would be a welcome addition to brighten up this sandwich.

Cumin Egg Salad Sandwich

8 eggs

1 tsp cumin seeds

¾ cup [180 g] full-fat yogurt

½ cup [10 g] cilantro leaves and tender stems, chopped

Kosher salt

Freshly ground black pepper

8 slices rustic bread

Olive oil

1 garlic clove, halved

8 large lettuce leaves

Makes 4 sandwiches • Bring a medium pot of water to a boil. Lower the eggs in and boil for 8 minutes. Remove from the pot and let sit at room temperature until cool enough to handle, then peel and roughly chop.

Meanwhile, in a small skillet over medium heat, toast the cumin seeds for 3 to 4 minutes, or until fragrant and barely darkened in color. Let cool.

In a large bowl, gently mix together the eggs, cumin seeds, yogurt, and cilantro, and season with salt and pepper. Eggs can take lots of salt, so don't be afraid to season liberally. Lightly toast the bread on a grill or under the broiler.

To assemble the sandwiches, drizzle the bread with olive oil and rub four pieces with the cut sides of the garlic clove halves. Place the lettuce leaves on the garlicky bread, spoon the egg salad over, season with more salt and pepper, and top with the remaining four slices of bread.

This is a substantial, no-fuss dish—perfect for when you have a big appetite. Save this for an evening after you've spent the day exploring outside and swimming in the sun and you need a filling meal. Use hearty greens, which keep for a longer time (about a week if refrigerated) and create a more robust texture in the stew.

Gingery Greens with Coconut Milk and Tofu

One 14 oz [400 g] package
extra-firm tofu

Kosher salt

2 or 3 bunches hearty greens,
like kale, chard, or collards
(about 1 lb [455 g])

3 Tbsp coconut oil

Freshly ground black pepper

2 medium onions, sliced

6 garlic cloves, thinly sliced

2 in [5 cm] piece of ginger,
peeled and thinly sliced into
matchsticks

One 13½ oz [400 ml] can
full-fat coconut milk

Juice of 1 lime

Cooked rice or rice noodles,
for serving

Makes 4 to 6 servings · Drain the tofu, place it on a kitchen towel, cover with another towel, and then set a cookie sheet with a weight on top. Let sit for about 30 minutes to press out the moisture. Cut the tofu into ¾ in [2 cm] cubes and set aside.

Meanwhile, bring a large pot of salted water to a boil. Blanch the greens until bright green and tender, about 5 minutes. Drain, cool slightly, and coarsely chop. Set aside.

In a large skillet over high heat, add 2 Tbsp of the coconut oil. Add the tofu, season with salt and pepper, and sear, turning once or twice, until the tofu cubes are brown on most sides. (Tofu will release itself from the skillet once it's nicely browned on the first side.) Transfer the tofu to a plate and set aside.

Turn the heat down to medium and add the remaining 1 Tbsp of coconut oil to the skillet. Add the onions, garlic, and ginger and cook until the onions are very soft and beginning to caramelize, about 20 minutes. Add the chopped greens, coconut milk, and lime juice, and season generously with salt and pepper. Bring to a simmer and let it bubble gently for about 10 minutes—longer if it seems very liquidy, shorter if it looks creamy before 10 minutes goes by. Nestle the cubed tofu in the greens and simmer for 5 minutes more. Serve with rice or rice noodles.

Simple, comforting, and reliable—this is my go-to dish. I have beans at home every week because both my baby and I love them so much. I really enjoy serving beans in broth; it makes the beans more tender, and I like soaking my bread in it.

Brothy Beans with Bread and Butter

1 lb [455 g] dry pinto, scarlet runner, navy, or cannellini beans (see Note)

A few rosemary sprigs

1 garlic head, halved crosswise

¼ cup [60 ml] olive oil, plus more as needed

Freshly ground black pepper

Kosher salt

Tender herbs, such as parsley, mint, or chives, roughly chopped, for serving

Lemon wedges, for serving

Good-quality bread and room-temperature salted butter, for serving

Makes 8 to 10 servings • Place the beans in a large pot and cover with several inches of water. Add the rosemary, garlic, olive oil, and lots of pepper. Bring to a boil, then immediately lower the heat and simmer; just a few bubbles should rise to the surface. Cook the beans for about 2 hours, seasoning with salt about halfway through. (Taste the cooking liquid at this point—it should be well seasoned, like pasta water.) The beans are done when they are completely tender; the skin should curl and peel when you blow on one, and the interior will be completely creamy and custardy, with no resistance when bitten. Add a bit more salt to the pot if the beans taste bland, as they will absorb seasoning as they cool in their liquid.

To serve, re-warm the beans in their liquid and fill bowls with beans and a few spoonfuls of their broth. Drizzle with olive oil, top with more pepper and chopped herbs, and serve with lemon wedges and bread and butter.

Note. You can soak the beans overnight to shorten the cooking time and make the beans easier to digest, but if the beans are fresh and heirloom, soaking is not necessary.

Carrots are usually a side dish, but adding feta and pistachios makes this recipe heartier and more filling. This recipe is also great with grilled carrots. If you choose to grill the carrots, keep them whole and grill them over high heat for 20 to 30 minutes. The carrots are ready when they are slightly brown and tender in the center when stabbed with a fork.

Maple-Glazed Carrots

¼ cup [60 ml] olive oil

1½ lb [680 g] carrots, peeled

Kosher salt

Freshly ground black pepper

Juice of 1 lemon

2 Tbsp maple syrup

1 garlic clove, grated

½ tsp red pepper flakes

¼ cup [5 g] parsley, chopped

2 oz [55 g] feta, crumbled

¼ cup [35 g] pistachios, chopped

Makes 4 servings • Preheat the oven to 425°F [220°C]. In a large ovenproof skillet, preferably cast iron, over medium-high heat, warm the olive oil. If your carrots are large, slice them on a bias about ¼ in [6 mm] thick; you can leave them whole if they're small. Add the carrots and season with salt and pepper, tossing occasionally, until the carrots become tender and begin to brown, about 10 minutes.

In a small bowl, mix together the lemon juice, maple syrup, garlic, and red pepper flakes, then add to the skillet. Toss to coat the carrots and cook for a few more minutes, tossing occasionally, until the sauce starts to thicken, then transfer the skillet to the oven.

Roast for 25 to 30 minutes, or until the carrots are deeply golden brown in spots and very tender. Remove from the oven, toss with the parsley, top with the feta and pistachios, and serve.

This stew is lightly inspired by the food my sailing mates and I ate on a trip to Greece. I like making it as a shared dish. I'll place the pot of stew in the middle of the dining table and let people serve themselves. Don't forget to offer some sourdough bread and butter on the side so you can soak up every last bit of stew from your bowl.

White Bean and Tomato Stew with Parmesan

¼ cup [60 ml] olive oil, plus more for serving

6 garlic cloves, thinly sliced

2 onions, sliced

Kosher salt

Freshly ground black pepper

1 Tbsp fennel seeds, lightly crushed in a mortar or with the side of a knife

½ cup [120 ml] white wine

One 28 oz [795 g] can whole tomatoes

1 Parmesan rind, plus ½ cup [15 g] grated, for serving

Two 15 oz [425 g] cans white beans (or 3 cups [480 g] cooked white beans and 1 cup [240 ml] cooking liquid)

1 cup [20 g] parsley, leaves and tender stems, for serving

Makes 4 to 6 servings • In a large pot over medium-high heat, warm the olive oil. Add the garlic and cook for 1 minute, stirring often, until the garlic is toasted and slightly golden. Immediately add the onions to stop the garlic from browning further, season with salt and pepper, and cook for 10 to 12 minutes, stirring occasionally, until the onions are soft but not browned.

Add the fennel seeds and cook for 1 minute. Add the wine and cook for about 5 minutes, or until mostly evaporated. Crush the tomatoes with your hands, then add them with their liquid and the Parmesan rind and season with salt and pepper. Bring to a boil, then lower the heat and simmer.

Cook for about 30 minutes, until the tomatoes are jammy, then add the beans and their liquid. Add 1½ cups [360 ml] of water (fill an empty bean can, which holds this amount). Increase the heat to bring it back to a simmer and cook for about 10 minutes, until the beans are heated through and the flavors have melded. Remove the Parmesan rind, taste for seasoning, and add salt as needed. Serve in bowls with a drizzle of olive oil, freshly ground black pepper, plenty of freshly grated Parmesan, and a sprinkling of parsley.

This is one of the most flavorful vegan meals I've ever had. The white wine lends a complex brightness to the tomato mixture, and the polenta made with lots of olive oil and bay leaf tastes decidedly of corn, in the best way. Warm any leftovers for breakfast, and top with fried eggs and lots of black pepper. This would be delicious with grated Parmesan or crumbled feta, but it doesn't need it.

Polenta with Garlicky Greens, Tomato, and Chickpeas

½ cup [120 ml] olive oil, plus more for serving

1 yellow onion, thinly sliced

6 garlic cloves, 5 crushed, 1 left whole

½ tsp red pepper flakes (optional)

Kosher salt

Freshly ground black pepper

One 15 oz [425 g] can chickpeas, drained

½ cup [120 ml] white wine

One 28 oz [795 g] can whole tomatoes

1 bunch kale, stemmed and chopped

1 cup [140 g] polenta

2 bay leaves

Makes 4 servings • In a medium pot over medium-high heat, warm ¼ cup [60 ml] of the olive oil. Add the onion, 5 crushed garlic cloves, and the red pepper flakes, if using. Season with salt and pepper and cook, stirring often, for about 15 minutes, or until the onion is soft and starting to brown in parts.

Add the chickpeas, season again with salt, and cook for about 5 minutes—the chickpeas may start to take on some color. Add the wine and let most of it cook off, which should take about 5 minutes. Crush the tomatoes with your hands, then add them with their juices to the pot. Season with salt again and simmer for about 30 minutes, until jammy.

Add the kale and a bit of water, if the sauce feels very thick, and season with more salt. Cover and simmer until the kale is tender, about 5 to 8 minutes. Grate the remaining garlic clove into the sauce, taste for seasoning, and remove from the heat.

While the sauce is simmering, make the polenta. Place the polenta in a heavy-bottomed medium pot with 4 cups [960 ml] of water, the bay leaves, the remaining ¼ cup [60 ml] of olive oil, and plenty of salt and pepper. Bring to a boil, then lower the heat and simmer, whisking constantly, until the polenta has thickened, 5 to 8 minutes. Continue simmering, stirring often and adding a little water if needed, for about 30 minutes. Taste the polenta. (Careful! It's very hot.) If the mouthfeel is gritty, it needs more time and probably a bit more water. If it's creamy and smoother than not, it's ready—just add more salt and pepper if needed. Discard the bay leaves and remove from the heat.

To serve, spoon the polenta evenly among four bowls. Top with the tomato-chickpea mixture, and drizzle with more olive oil and plenty of cracked black pepper.

This recipe is very versatile because almost any leftovers can go in here, such as cooked greens, carrots, mushrooms, tofu, sausage, or shrimp. It's the perfect end-of-trip, clean-out-your-fridge kind of meal. Use this recipe as a base, and feel free to add more ingredients depending on what you like and have on hand. I like to put it in to-go containers and take it to the beach with a bottle of white wine to watch the last sunset of the trip.

Leftover Fried Rice

2 Tbsp neutral oil, such as grapeseed

2 medium carrots, peeled and chopped

2 celery stalks, chopped

1 onion, chopped

6 garlic cloves, smashed

1 in [2.5 cm] piece of ginger, grated

Kosher salt

2 eggs

Soy sauce, to taste

1 tsp sesame oil

2 cups [240 g] cooked white rice

Rice vinegar, to taste

2 scallions, white and light green parts, thinly sliced, for serving

Toasted sesame seeds, for serving

Hot sauce, like sambal or sriracha, for serving

Makes 4 servings • In a large skillet over medium-high heat, warm the oil. Add the carrot, celery, onion, garlic, and ginger and season with salt. Cook the vegetables until just tender, stirring often, about 10 minutes.

Meanwhile, whisk the eggs in a medium bowl and season with a bit of soy sauce. Move the vegetables to the perimeter of the skillet, making a well in the center. Add the sesame oil and then the eggs to the well and stir constantly until a soft scramble forms.

Add the rice to the skillet and stir together the rice, eggs, and vegetables. Cook until the rice has heated through, about 5 minutes. Season with more soy sauce and a splash of vinegar. Remove from the heat, top with scallions and sesame seeds, and serve with hot sauce.

This is one of my all-time favorite meals. It's filling, delicious, and absolutely beautiful. Rice is my starch of choice—it helps ease queasy stomachs at sea, keeps you full for a long time, and is such a versatile base. I love adding young pickled vegetables to this dish (see page 112). This is also a great boat or beach meal since the whole thing is served in a bowl—easy to eat and minimal cleanup!

Siren Bowl

Rice Bowl

1 cup [200 g] black forbidden rice

Kosher salt

Splash of apple cider vinegar

2 eggs

½ tsp ground turmeric

Miso Tahini Dressing

¼ cup [55 g] tahini

2 Tbsp miso paste

1 garlic clove, grated

1 in [2.5 cm] piece of ginger, grated

Juice of ½ lemon

For serving

1 large or 2 small radishes, thinly sliced

1 carrot, cut into ribbons with a vegetable peeler

½ avocado, thinly sliced

Pinch of hemp seeds

Torn cilantro leaves

Red pepper flakes

Makes 2 servings • **To make the rice bowl:** In a medium saucepan with a tight-fitting lid over medium heat, bring 1½ cups [360 ml] of water to a boil. Add the rice and a pinch of salt. Bring to a simmer, cover, and cook for 25 minutes. Without lifting the lid, remove from the heat and let the rice steam for 8 minutes. Fluff the rice. If there is still any water at the bottom of the pan, place back over low heat with the lid off for another 1 to 2 minutes, until the water evaporates.

Line a plate with a paper towel. In a large saucepan, add enough water to come up the sides about 2 in [5 cm]. Add the vinegar and bring to a simmer. Meanwhile, crack the eggs into separate ramekins or small bowls. Stir the turmeric into the simmering water. Using a slotted spoon, stir the water in one direction and gently drop an egg into the whirlpool. Keep the water moving around the egg so the whites of the egg wrap around the yolk. Cook the egg, stirring constantly, for 3 minutes. Carefully transfer the egg to the prepared plate and repeat with the second egg.

To make the miso tahini dressing: In a medium bowl, whisk together the tahini, miso, garlic, ginger, and lemon juice. If the mixture is too thick, slowly add in some hot tap water until you achieve the desired consistency.

To serve: Spoon some rice into the bottom of each bowl. Top each with the eggs, radish, carrot, avocado, hemp seeds, cilantro, and red pepper flakes. Sprinkle everything with a dusting of salt and serve with the dressing.

Pirate Talk

Here is some basic seafaring lingo that will make you sound like a real sailor:

Chow down
Let's eat!

Old salt
A sailor with lots of experience at sea; a well-seasoned traveler.

Feeling blue
If a captain died at sea, the crew would fly a blue flag, and with time, this phrase equated to feeling sad.

Mayday or M'aidez *(French)*
Help me!

Through thick and thin
For better or worse! Originates from a method of pulling thin and thick ropes to hoist a sail.

Three sheets to the wind
Drunk; someone who has had one too many drinks.

Pipe down
Be quiet! This saying comes from back in the day, when a boatswain would use a pipe to signify that sailors should retire to the hammocks below deck and rest.

Make waves
Cause trouble.

All hands on deck
This is a call to action; everyone needs to help.

Abandon ship
Leave the situation.

Sundown Hour

Here is a refreshing mocktail with a little spice that can be made at any time of day. I like it in the morning to settle my stomach, or in the late afternoon in place of a cocktail. With ginger, bubbly water, and a squeeze of citrus over the top, it's an invigorating alternative if you don't feel like drinking alcohol.

Ginger Turmeric Sparkling Water

4 in [10 cm] piece of ginger, grated

4 in [10 cm] piece of turmeric, grated (or 1 tsp ground turmeric)

½ cup [100 g] brown sugar

Sparkling water, for serving

Lemon or lime wedge, for garnish

Makes 8 drinks • In a small pot over high heat, warm the ginger, turmeric, brown sugar, and 2 cups [480 ml] of water. Bring to a boil, then lower the heat and gently simmer for 15 minutes. Strain the syrup into a 1 pt [475 ml] glass jar and let cool, then cover and refrigerate for up to 1 week.

To serve, shake the jar well and add approximately 2 Tbsp of the syrup mixture to 8 oz [240 ml] of sparkling water, or to taste. Garnish with a wedge of lemon.

This cocktail takes a little bit of preparation, but the juice is worth the squeeze! A twist on the classic margarita, this recipe uses a milk clarification process that has been around for hundreds of years. Because this cocktail is shelf-stable, it's the perfect companion for your seaside journey. I recommend making a large batch in advance and saving it for a beautiful sunset.

Clarified Margarita

2 oz [60 ml] tequila

1 oz [30 ml] fresh lime juice

1 oz [30 ml] simple syrup (50:50 ratio)

1 oz [30 ml] whole milk

Makes 1 drink • In a cocktail shaker or glass, mix together the tequila, lime juice, and simple syrup. In a second glass, add the whole milk. Pour the tequila mixture into the milk (make sure to do it this way, instead of pouring the milk into the tequila mixture). Let it rest for at least 5 minutes. The acid will curdle the milk, separating the curds and whey.

Pour the curdled mixture through a coffee filter or a cheesecloth set over a third glass or a mason jar. This part takes a little while, about 1 hour. Bottle the liquid to take on your journey, or pour it over ice to serve and enjoy.

This cocktail has floral and bitter notes, and a little spice from the ginger. If you're making multiple drinks at once, save time by making a batch of equal parts Salers Aperitif and blanc vermouth. Top off individual glasses with ginger beer before serving.

French Americano

1 oz [30 ml] Salers Aperitif

1 oz [30 ml] blanc vermouth

Ginger beer, for serving

Lemon peel, for garnish

Makes 1 drink • In a highball or stemless wineglass filled with ice, add the Salers Aperitif and blanc vermouth. Top off with ginger beer, garnish with a lemon peel, and serve.

Originally from Cuba, this is my favorite drink to sip on the beach! You can add a little less simple syrup if you'd prefer a less-sweet version.

Classic Daiquiri

2 oz [60 ml] good-quality rum

1 oz [30 ml] fresh lime juice

1 oz [30 ml] simple syrup (50:50 ratio)

Makes 1 drink • In a mason jar, combine the rum, lime juice, and simple syrup. Throw in a handful of ice, close the lid, and shake vigorously. (Make this your arm workout for the day!) Strain the drink into a highball glass or another mason jar, sans ice, and serve.

This is a flexible recipe; feel free to add more vegetables or swap in others you have on hand. Cauliflower florets and green beans work well. Note that if you use a vegetable with color, it will likely bleed into the rest of the ingredients in the jar. I like to use these pickled vegetables on Sardine Toast (page 158), or use on any sandwich of your liking.

Overnight Pickles with Lemon and Seaweed

1 cup [240 ml] unseasoned rice vinegar

1 Tbsp plus 1 tsp granulated sugar

1 Tbsp plus 1 tsp kosher salt

Zest of 2 lemons

½ tsp dried kelp granules

2 medium carrots, peeled and thinly sliced

1 yellow onion, thinly sliced into rings

1 cucumber, peeled and thinly sliced

Makes about 1 pt [475 g] • In a 1 pt [475 ml] jar, mix together the vinegar, sugar, salt, lemon zest, and kelp. Add the vegetables, cover the jar, shake, and refrigerate overnight. Pickles will be ready in 8 to 12 hours and will keep, refrigerated, for 1 week.

For the best guacamole, make sure your avocados are ripe but not too ripe! If the avocados need a little help ripening, place them in a brown bag for a few hours; it will expedite the process. If only there were such an easy trick to save the overripe ones!

Guacamole

½ tsp ground cumin

1 garlic clove, minced

1 small shallot, minced

1 jalapeño, minced

Juice of 2 limes, plus more as needed

Kosher salt

Freshly ground black pepper

3 ripe avocados, halved and pitted

½ cup [10 g] cilantro, finely chopped

Makes 4 to 6 servings • In a medium skillet set over medium heat, toast the cumin, shaking the skillet occasionally, until very fragrant and maybe starting to take on a bit of color, about 5 minutes. Let cool.

In a medium bowl, mix together the garlic, shallot, jalapeño, and lime juice and season very generously with salt and pepper. Let sit for 5 to 10 minutes, then add the avocado and mix well with a fork, mashing the avocado to your preferred texture. Add the cumin and cilantro, mix well, taste for salt and lime, and season as needed. Serve immediately.

A mishmash of two of my daughter's favorite things to eat: hummus and petit pois (green peas)! I love serving this healthy-yummy dip with slices of endive, raw cucumbers, and salty chips.

Very Green Pea Hummus

1 cup [120 g] green peas, fresh or frozen

1 cup [160 g] cooked or canned chickpeas

¼ cup [55 g] tahini

1 garlic clove, grated or minced

Zest and juice of 1 lemon

Kosher salt

Freshly ground black pepper

½ cup [20 g] mixed fresh herbs, such as parsley, cilantro, mint, or basil

2 Tbsp olive oil, plus more for serving

2 Tbsp cold water

Makes 2 cups [455 g] • If you're using frozen peas, thaw them overnight in the fridge or briefly rinse them with warm water.

Place the peas, chickpeas, tahini, garlic, lemon zest and juice, several pinches of salt, and several grinds of black pepper in a blender or food processor. Blend until a chunky mixture forms, about 1 minute, and then add the herbs and olive oil. Continue to blend until the mixture starts to become smooth, 1 to 2 minutes. With the motor running, add the cold water and continue to blend until it's as smooth as you like—anywhere from 1 to 3 minutes, depending on the strength of your food processor and the texture you prefer. Taste for salt and pepper and season as needed.

Transfer the hummus to a wide bowl, swooshing it with a spoon into pretty swirls, and then drizzle with more olive oil. Serve with crunchy vegetables or Easy Bake Sumac Crackers (page 117).

Watch the *sunrise* and *sunset* whenever you can. If I ever feel disconnected from nature, I watch the sunset and instantly feel better. Being awake for sunrise also helps your body tune in with your *circadian rhythm*. This is a great natural way to help beat jet lag and cure sleepless nights. Just another example of how our bodies are *connected* to our environment.

Why make a cracker from scratch when there are dozens of options on hand at every grocery store in the world, you ask? Because sometimes special moments call for special snacks. These crackers are foolproof, flavorful, and unexpected. Scatter their irregular shapes next to a wedge of salty cheese and a bowl of olives at sundown.

Easy Bake Sumac Crackers

1½ cups [210 g] all-purpose flour, plus more for dusting

½ cup [120 ml] cold water

2 Tbsp olive oil

1 Tbsp ground sumac

1 tsp kosher salt

Makes 4 to 6 servings • In a large bowl, combine all the ingredients, mixing thoroughly with your hands or a wooden spoon. Dump the dough onto a clean counter or large cutting board and knead briefly, 1 to 2 minutes, to fully bring together into a shaggy mass. Cover the dough with a clean cloth and let rest for about 30 minutes.

Meanwhile, preheat the oven to 425°F [220°C].

Lightly flour the work surface and roll out the dough until it is very thin and approximately 18 by 13 in [46 by 33 cm]—it should just about fill a half sheet tray. If the dough is resisting you and pulling back, you may need to let it rest for a few more minutes before you try rolling it out again. Spread the dough onto the sheet tray, prick it all over with a fork, and bake for 20 minutes, rotating the pan halfway through, or until the cracker is beautifully golden brown. Let cool completely, then break into pieces. Store in an airtight container for up to 4 days.

Deviled eggs are a classic appetizer. They are easy to transport too—bring them to a beach house potluck or a cocktail hour on someone else's boat. I recommend serving them with a nice glass of crisp Alsace Riesling.

Spicy Deviled Eggs

12 eggs

¼ cup [60 g] mayonnaise

¼ cup [5 g] finely chopped cilantro leaves

¼ cup [40 g] finely chopped pickled jalapeños

½ tsp cayenne

½ tsp smoked paprika

Kosher salt

Freshly ground black pepper

Aleppo pepper or red pepper flakes, for serving (optional)

Makes 24 halves • Bring a large pot of water to a boil and gently add the eggs; boil for 9 minutes. Transfer the eggs immediately to a bowl of ice water. When they're fully cool, peel and halve the eggs. Remove the yolks from the eggs, placing them in a medium bowl. Arrange the whites on a large tray or platter and set aside.

Mix the yolks in the bowl with the mayonnaise, cilantro, pickled jalapeños, cayenne, and smoked paprika until well combined. Season with salt and pepper.

Season the egg whites with salt, then spoon the yolk mixture into the whites—using two spoons works well, or use a piping bag if you're feeling fancy. Sprinkle the aleppo pepper on top, if using. Serve immediately.

Ceviche is so refreshing, with its punchy combination of lime and heat. Although most ceviche includes fresh fish, I prefer mine unconventional. But if you'd like to lean more traditional, feel free to add high-quality white fish or shrimp to this recipe (see Note). I imagine you making this with salt in your hair and a nice tan line from a day spent outside.

Vegetable Ceviche with Coco Leche de Tigre

½ **jicama, peeled and diced**

1 **medium English cucumber, diced**

1 **bunch radishes, diced**

1 **pint [340 g] cherry tomatoes, quartered**

6 **limes**

Kosher salt

½ **red onion, finely diced**

1 **jalapeño, seeded and diced**

1 **cup [240 ml] light coconut milk**

2 **Tbsp honey**

1 **cup [20 g] cilantro leaves and tender stems**

Tortilla chips, for serving

Makes 6 to 8 servings as an appetizer • Place the jicama, cucumber, radishes, and cherry tomatoes in a large bowl. Zest 2 of the limes and squeeze their juice over the top. Season very liberally with salt, toss, and set aside.

Place the onion, jalapeño, and juice of the remaining 4 limes in a medium bowl and season with salt. Let sit for at least 15 minutes. Stir in the coconut milk and honey; this is the coco leche de tigre. Place the vegetables and their liquid into a wide serving bowl, pour the coco leche de tigre over the top, and sprinkle with the cilantro. Serve with tortilla chips.

Note. This would be delicious with the addition of shrimp or fish. To add shrimp, stir in ¼ lb [115 g] of chopped cooked shrimp right before plating the vegetables in the serving bowl. Or you could prepare raw shrimp in classic ceviche manner: Add salt and lime juice to the raw shrimp and let sit for 30 minutes to 1 hour. Keep the shrimp separate from the vegetables until the last minute; the water released from the vegetables would dilute the lime juice too much and prevent the shrimp from properly "cooking." To add fish, cut ¾ lb [340 g] of high-quality white fish into ½ in [13 mm] cubes, season with salt, and let it marinate in lime juice for about 20 minutes before adding it to the ceviche.

Making bread from scratch can be tricky, especially if you can't control the temperatures in your kitchen. These flatbreads are an excellent alternative; they're reliable to make and, because they're chemically leavened with baking soda (rather than yeast), they don't need much kneading. They make a great vessel for dipping into Very Green Pea Hummus (page 115) and other dips.

The Easiest Grilled Flatbread

2 cups [280 g] all-purpose flour, plus more for dusting

1½ tsp kosher salt

½ tsp baking soda

1 cup [240 g] full-fat yogurt

1 tsp apple cider vinegar

Olive oil

Flaky sea salt

Makes four 8 to 10 in [20 to 25 cm] flatbreads • In a large bowl, mix together the flour, kosher salt, and baking soda. Add the yogurt and vinegar and mix well until a shaggy dough forms. Dust a work surface with a bit of flour, knead the dough briefly to bring it together, 2 to 3 minutes, then divide it into four balls and place them on the work surface. Cover the dough with a clean kitchen towel and let rest for 20 minutes and up to 1 hour.

Prepare a grill for high heat. Using more flour as needed, roll each piece of dough into a circle roughly 8 to 10 in [20 to 25 cm] in diameter. Brush off any excess flour and grill the dough rounds for about 3 minutes per side, moving the dough around a bit to allow for even heating. When the flatbreads come off the grill, drizzle with olive oil and sprinkle with flaky salt.

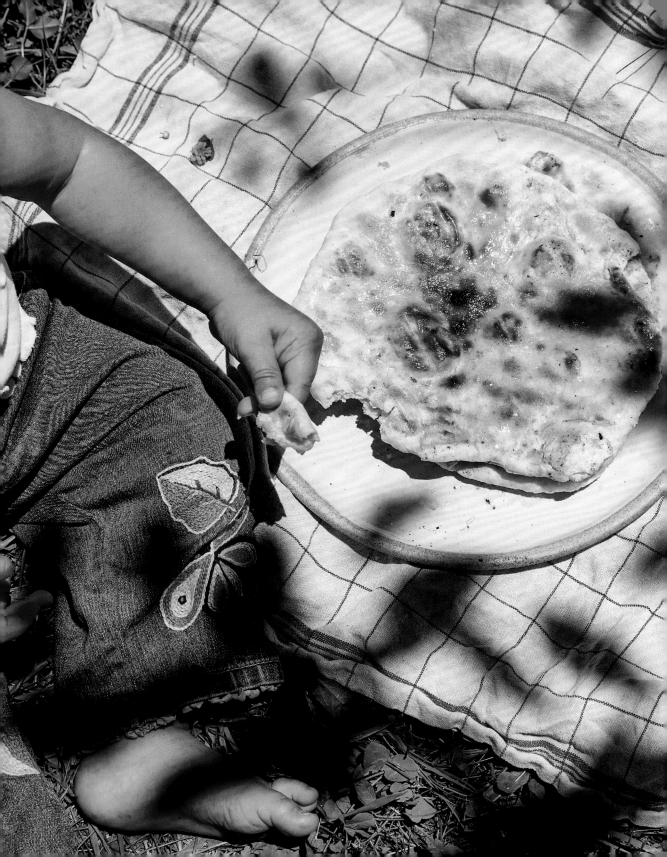

A few years back, I was on a sailboat in *Greece* with some of my best friends, docked at a small island. As the *sun was setting*, I made a bed on the bow of the boat, as I usually prefer to *sleep under the stars* instead of in the cabin.

There was a restaurant nearby that started a *beautiful show of fireworks*. We were all very excited to watch the show from the boat. Little did we know it was the beginning of a Greek wedding celebration that would. Not. End. The music seemed to grow louder and louder throughout the night. The party finally ended with the bride and groom *jumping into the ocean* fully clothed at sunrise!

Traveling may not *always* be easy or comfortable, but it is so *worthwhile*, and you'll make amazing memories!

I love Japanese sweet potatoes; I feel like we always have a couple baking in the oven at my house (and often I forget and leave them in there). This miso-roasted version is my rendition of a dish served at NYC restaurant Momofuku.

Miso-Roasted Japanese Sweet Potato with Spicy Mayo

Miso-Roasted Sweet Potatoes

¼ cup [50 g] white miso paste

¼ cup [60 ml] neutral oil, such as grapeseed

1 Tbsp plus 1 tsp maple syrup

1 Tbsp plus 1 tsp soy sauce

1 tsp kosher salt

1 garlic clove, grated

4 medium Japanese sweet potatoes (about 2½ lb [1.1 kg]), cut into wedges

Flaky sea salt

Spicy Mayo

1 cup [240 g] mayonnaise (store-bought or homemade, page 81)

2 Tbsp gochujang or yuzu kosho

2 scallions, thinly sliced

1 tsp toasted sesame seeds

Makes 6 to 8 servings • To make the miso-roasted sweet potatoes: Preheat the oven to 425°F [220°C]. In a large bowl, whisk together the miso paste, oil, maple syrup, soy sauce, kosher salt, and garlic until combined. Add the sweet potatoes and toss well until thoroughly coated. Spread the sweet potatoes out on a large baking sheet, using two if necessary to avoid crowding. Roast for 25 to 30 minutes, or until the sweet potatoes are golden brown and tender. Garnish with flaky salt before serving.

To make the spicy mayo: In a medium bowl, mix together the mayonnaise and gochujang. Top with the scallions and sesame seeds, and serve it alongside the sweet potatoes.

You can make a party out of this recipe: Prepare the veggies, noodles, and dipping sauce beforehand, and then let guests build their own rolls. Make sure everyone gets at least two tries—rolling the wrappers tightly takes a bit of practice. But not to worry! They'll taste refreshing and delicious no matter the outcome.

Fresh Vietnamese-Style Spring Rolls

3 oz [85 g] rice vermicelli

1 tsp toasted sesame oil

Kosher salt

8 spring roll wrappers (rice paper)

1 cup [20 g] fresh herbs, such as cilantro, mint, Thai basil, or shiso

1 cup [30 g] torn lettuce leaves

1 cup [60 g] thinly sliced cabbage (red cabbage looks nice but green works too)

2 medium carrots, peeled and thinly cut into matchsticks

1 medium cucumber, peeled, seeded, and thinly cut into matchsticks

1 medium daikon radish, thinly cut into matchsticks

1 recipe Peanut Sauce (page 75), for serving

Hot sauce, such as sambal or sriracha, for serving

Makes 8 rolls • Cook the vermicelli according to the package instructions. Drain, rinse under cold water, and toss in a medium bowl with the sesame oil and a pinch of salt. Set aside.

Fill a shallow pan, like a 9 in [23 cm] square cake pan, with warm water. Use a clean cutting board as your work surface, and begin assembling: Dunk a single rice paper in the pan of water, submerging it completely for 20 to 30 seconds or until it is just pliable but still fairly stiff. It will continue to soften as you assemble the roll. (Knowing the right time to pull the wrapper from the water takes a bit of practice—luckily, you will almost certainly have extra rice papers!)

Remove the rice paper, shake off the excess water, and lay it flat on the cutting board. Lay a few herb leaves on the bottom third of the rice paper. Top with a lettuce leaf or two, a small pile of rice noodles, cabbage, carrots, cucumber, daikon, and more herbs if you like. Fold the top third of the wrap over the vegetables, tightly tuck in the sides, and roll the rest of the way. Repeat with the remaining rice papers. Serve with the peanut sauce and hot sauce.

Buying Wine Abroad

I believe the key to finding good wine abroad is finding local wine shops. I've found that the smaller the wine shop, the more the owner will curate the selections. Every wine will be handpicked based on quality, rather than available quantity. The larger the wine shop, the more the quality usually wavers, as the range is larger. Speak to the owner and employees to get their recommendations—they know better than anyone. In my experience, you can find a nice bottle of wine for $20 to $30 in the United States, and 10 to 20 euros in Europe. That seems to be the sweet spot for high-quality wines that don't break the bank. And if all else fails, pick a cool label!

Hearty Meals to Share

Nuoc cham is a brilliant sauce that hails from Vietnam, composed of fish sauce, sugar, water, lime juice, and often chiles and garlic. In this version, because its purpose is to douse vegetables as soon as they come off the grill, the water is omitted—there's plenty of moisture in the eggplant and kale, and bold flavors are the goal here. While perfectly grilled eggplant and kale need little else than salt and a touch of acid, they are made transcendent with the addictive flavors of nuoc cham and the abundance of herbs.

Grilled Eggplant and Kale with Nuoc Cham

Nuoc Cham

¼ cup [60 ml] lime juice

3 Tbsp dark brown sugar

3 Tbsp fish sauce

1 garlic clove, grated or minced

1 small Thai chile, such as bird's eye, minced, or 1 tsp minced fresh jalapeño

Grilled Vegetables

2 bunches kale, stemmed

2 medium eggplants, sliced lengthwise into ½ in [2 cm] thick slabs

¼ cup [60 ml] neutral oil, such as grapeseed

Kosher salt

Freshly ground black pepper

For serving

Cooked rice noodles or rice

1 cup [20 g] mixed herbs, such as mint, Thai basil, cilantro, or shiso, torn

½ cup [70 g] chopped roasted peanuts

Makes 4 servings • **To make the nuoc cham:** In a medium bowl or mason jar, mix together the lime juice, brown sugar, fish sauce, garlic, and chile. Set aside.

To grill the vegetables: Prepare a grill for medium heat. Spread whole kale leaves and eggplant slabs on a rimmed baking sheet, drizzle with the oil, and season with salt and pepper. With your hands, make sure the kale and eggplant are evenly coated in oil. Grill the kale leaves first, 1 to 2 minutes per side—you're just looking for a bit of char. Grill the eggplant next, turning the

slabs occasionally, until well browned on both sides and very tender, about 15 minutes total. (It's more important to take the eggplant to the place where it's deliciously browned and the flesh has collapsed than it is to look at the clock.) Roughly chop the kale and transfer with the eggplant to a large bowl. Add about half of the nuoc cham, mix well, and taste. Continue to add nuoc cham as needed, to taste.

To serve: Lay the vegetables over rice noodles in wide bowls, and top with torn herbs and roasted peanuts.

When I was in Thailand for three weeks, I lived off of this soup with a side of morning glory (a type of water spinach common to Southeast Asia). I couldn't get enough: The balance of the sweet, rich coconut milk and the spice from the curry is so delicious. Still to this day, when I make this recipe, I am taken back to those days—eating this dish in a humble restaurant in a small alley in Bangkok.

Veggie Khao Soi

Curry Paste

2 dried chiles

2 cups [480 ml] boiling water

4 garlic cloves

2 shallots, peeled

1 in [2.5 cm] piece of ginger

1 Tbsp ground coriander

2 tsp ground turmeric

2 tsp curry powder

¼ tsp ground cardamom

Zest of 2 limes

½ bunch cilantro, stems only

Soup

2 Tbsp neutral oil, such as grapeseed

2 medium onions, sliced

Two 13½ oz [400 ml] cans full-fat coconut milk

4 medium carrots, peeled and chopped

1 cauliflower, broken into florets

Kosher salt

1 bunch kale, stemmed and chopped

Juice of 2 limes, plus 6 lime wedges, for serving

12 oz [340 g] rice noodles, cooked according to package instructions

Cilantro, for garnish

Makes 6 servings • To make the curry paste: In a large bowl, soak the dried chiles in the water for 30 minutes. Strain, reserving the soaking liquid. Add all of the ingredients to a blender or food processor, add 2 Tbsp of the chile soaking liquid, and blend on high speed until smooth, using more soaking liquid as needed to make a smooth paste. Set aside.

To make the soup: In a Dutch oven or other large, wide-bottomed pot over medium heat, warm the oil. Add the onions and cook for 10 minutes, or until the onions are soft but not brown. Add

the curry paste and cook for 5 minutes, until the paste is fragrant. Add the coconut milk, carrots, cauliflower, and 1½ cups [360 ml] of water (you can fill the coconut milk can) and season with salt. Bring to a boil, then lower the heat and simmer until the cauliflower and carrots are just tender, about 10 minutes. Add the kale and cook until wilted, about 5 minutes. Add the lime juice and taste for seasoning, adding salt as needed.

To serve: Spoon the rice noodles into individual bowls and top with the soup. Scatter cilantro leaves over each bowl and serve with lime wedges.

This is a pantry pasta for the nights when the sun is setting, the markets are closed, and a hunger pang is your cue that it's time to make dinner. It comes together quickly and uses ingredients you likely have on hand. The simple trick of blanching greens and cooking pasta in the same pot of salted water will result in a beautifully green, bright, and silky bowl of noodles. Use any nut you have on hand, any bunch of greens, and any hard, salty cheese. Lemon and salt are your only nonnegotiables!

Pasta with Walnuts, Chiles, and Greens

Kosher salt

¼ cup [60 ml] plus 2 Tbsp olive oil, plus more for serving

1 cup [120 g] walnuts, crushed

4 garlic cloves, crushed

1 fresh chile, thinly sliced, or 1 tsp red pepper flakes

Freshly ground black pepper

1 lemon, zest reserved, seeded, peeled, and roughly chopped

1 bunch greens, such as kale, Swiss chard, or mustard greens, stemmed

1 lb [455 g] short pasta, such as rigatoni

Shaved Parmesan cheese, for serving

Makes 4 to 6 servings • Bring a large pot of well-salted water to a boil. Meanwhile, in a large, wide skillet or Dutch oven over medium-high heat, warm the olive oil. Add the walnuts, garlic, and chile and season with salt and pepper. Cook for about 6 minutes, stirring often, or until the walnuts are toasted and the garlic is golden and fragrant. Add the chopped lemon and cook for 1 minute. Turn the heat to low and let cook for about 10 minutes, stirring occasionally.

Blanch the greens in the salted boiling water for 2 to 3 minutes, or until tender and bright green, then strain out the leaves with a spider or large slotted spoon. When the greens are cool enough to handle, chop them into bite-size pieces and set aside.

Cook the pasta in the same pot of water until almost al dente, stopping 2 or 3 minutes before it's cooked to your liking. Strain the pasta out of the water and place directly into the skillet with the walnut mixture. Add pasta water a ½ cup [120 ml] (or ladleful) at a time, tossing the pasta well in between each scoop until the liquid is mostly absorbed and the pasta is perfectly al dente. Add the chopped greens and toss for 1 minute.

Taste for seasoning, then divide the pasta among bowls, or transfer to a large serving platter, drizzle with olive oil, and sprinkle with the lemon zest and Parmesan.

I first made this on a boat off the coast of Thailand somewhere. The langoustines were from a fisherman who brought his boat up alongside ours to sell his most recent catch. He told me how to prepare it, and it was a hit! I hope you enjoy it too.

Lime and Chile Grilled Shrimp

4 garlic cloves, grated

1 serrano or Thai chile, minced

Juice of 3 limes, plus 1 cut into wedges, for serving

2 Tbsp dark brown sugar

2 Tbsp fish sauce

1 lb [455 g] head-on shrimp or langoustines

2 cups [240 g] cooked white rice, for serving

1 cup [20 g] mixed sprigs of herbs, such as mint, cilantro, or Thai basil, for serving

Makes 4 servings • In a medium bowl, mix together the garlic, chile, lime juice, brown sugar, and fish sauce. Add the shrimp and toss to coat. Let marinate unrefrigerated for 30 minutes, or refrigerated for up to 1 hour.

Prepare a grill for high heat. Place a small, grill-safe pot on one corner of the grill. Set a clean medium bowl and a sturdy pot holder (or thick, dry folded kitchen towel) near the grill. Lift the shrimp out of the marinade with tongs, shaking off any excess liquid, and place them directly on the grill. Cook for 2 minutes per side, or until opaque and slightly charred.

Meanwhile, carefully pour the marinade into the pot. It will foam a bit upon contact with the hot pan, and then immediately come to a simmer. Let it reduce while the shrimp cook. When the shrimp are done, place them into the clean bowl and carefully pour the marinade, using the pot holder, over the shrimp. Toss to coat. Serve with rice, herbs, and lime wedges.

This dish is a celebration of summer, with lots of herbs that add floral, vegetal complexity and lemon that brings bitterness for depth and acid for brightness. Use shrimp if you can get them (have the fishmonger peel and devein them for you, if you like) or keep it vegetarian; both versions are satisfying.

Lemon and Herb Pasta with Shrimp

¼ cup [60 ml] olive oil

3 shallots, chopped

3 garlic cloves, crushed

½ tsp red pepper flakes (optional)

Kosher salt

Freshly ground black pepper

1 lb [455 g] shrimp, peeled and deveined (optional)

1 lb [455 g] pasta of any shape

Zest and juice of 1 lemon

1 packed cup [20 g] mixed herbs, such as parsley, basil, and mint, chopped

2 Tbsp unsalted butter

Makes 4 servings • In a large, heavy-bottomed pot like a Dutch oven or a wide skillet over medium heat, warm the olive oil. Add the shallot, garlic, and red pepper flakes, if using, and season with salt and pepper. Cook for about 10 minutes, until the shallot starts to gently caramelize. If using shrimp, add them now, season with salt, and cook until they just turn pink, tossing frequently, about 5 minutes. Remove from the heat.

Meanwhile, bring a large pot of well-salted water to a boil over high heat and cook the pasta until almost al dente, stopping 2 to 3 minutes before it's cooked to your liking. Strain the pasta from the water using tongs or a spider strainer, depending on the shape of your pasta, and place the pasta directly into the pot with the shallots and shrimp. Add about ½ cup [120 ml] of pasta water to the pot and toss until the sauce is glossy and the pasta is cooked through. Finely chop the lemon zest and add it along with the lemon juice. Add the herbs and butter, toss well, taste and adjust for seasoning, and serve.

Slow-cooking squid makes them tender beyond belief. This spicy tomato sauce absorbs some of their salinity, resulting in a delicious and surprising dish. Make the squid-tomato sauce ahead of time and warm it up on the boat—then all you have to do is boil some pasta and chop some herbs.

Slow-Cooked Spicy Squid with Pasta and Herbs

1½ lb [680 g] squid, bodies and tentacles, cleaned

One 28 oz [795 g] can whole tomatoes

¼ cup [60 ml] olive oil

1 onion, diced

4 garlic cloves, crushed

1 Tbsp coriander seeds, lightly crushed in a mortar or with the side of a knife

1 tsp red pepper flakes, or to taste

½ cup [120 ml] white wine

Kosher salt

Freshly ground black pepper

1 lb [455 g] short pasta, such as gemelli or rigatoni

½ cup [10 g] mixed herbs, such as parsley, mint, basil, or dill, finely chopped

1 lemon, cut into wedges, for serving

Makes 6 to 8 servings • Slice the squid bodies into rings about ¼ in [6 mm] thick; leave the tentacles as is. Set aside.

In a medium bowl, crush the tomatoes with your hands. Set aside.

In a large, heavy-bottomed pot or Dutch oven over medium heat, warm the olive oil. Add the onion and garlic and cook for 10 to 12 minutes, stirring often, until soft but not browned.

Add the coriander seeds and red pepper flakes and cook for 1 minute, until fragrant. Add the wine and bring to a simmer for 1 minute. Pour the tomatoes and their juices into the pot along with the squid, then season with salt and pepper. Bring to a simmer, then turn the heat to low, cover, and

cook until the squid is very tender, 1 to 1½ hours. The squid will release some liquid, so if the sauce looks too brothy, simmer uncovered for 10 to 15 minutes to let it thicken a bit while you cook the pasta.

Meanwhile, bring a large pot of generously salted water to a boil. Cook the pasta until almost al dente, stopping 2 to 3 minutes before it's cooked to your liking, then strain it out of the water with tongs or a slotted spoon, depending on the shape of your pasta, and add it directly to the pot with the squid. Toss continuously for 1 to 2 minutes, or until the sauce is glossy and the pasta is al dente. Divide the pasta, squid, and sauce among individual bowls or serve in a large serving bowl. Top with the herbs and serve with lemon wedges on the side.

This dish is très français. You might be familiar with moules frites; well, this is a version of it. I would accompany this dish with a nice sourdough bread and some room-temperature butter on the side to dip in the sauce.

Mussels with Beer, Mustard, and Herbs

2 lb [910 g] mussels

2 Tbsp olive oil

1 onion, diced

10 to 12 sprigs parsley, stems finely chopped, leaves coarsely chopped

1 cup [240 ml] beer (any mellow ale or lager will work)

2 Tbsp coarse-ground mustard

2 Tbsp unsalted butter

Kosher salt, to taste

½ bunch chives, finely chopped

Good bread and salted butter, for serving

Makes 2 servings as a main course, 4 as an appetizer • Scrub the mussels, pulling off any beards (the ropey stuff along the seams) and discarding any that have opened. (You can also purchase mussels already cleaned to save a step.) Set aside.

In a large, shallow pot or Dutch oven over medium heat, warm the olive oil. Add the onion and parsley stems and cook for 5 minutes, or until the onion is soft but not browned. Add the beer, mustard, unsalted butter, and mussels and bring to a simmer. Cover and cook for 5 minutes, or until the mussels have all opened. Discard any that don't open; if you are cooking this on a boat, feel free to toss the unopened mussels in the ocean.

Transfer the mussels to shallow bowls, leaving the broth in the pot. Season the broth with salt to taste, then pour the broth over the mussels in bowls and sprinkle the parsley leaves and chives over the top. Serve with bread and salted butter.

This broth is as *satisfying* as the mussels themselves. One of my *favorite indulgences* is dipping buttered bread into it, or even *drinking it* by the spoonful!

I like to serve this fish in a dish alongside the warmed tortillas and toppings and let people make their own tacos. Guacamole (page 113) and Grilled Corn Salad (page 78) are perfect sides to make this into a bigger meal. Whip up a big pitcher of Clarified Margaritas (page 108) and you have yourself a dinner party in the making. I hope your feet are sandy while enjoying these.

Fish Tacos

¼ cup [50 g] chipotles in adobo

½ cup [120 g] mayonnaise

1 garlic clove, grated

2 cups [120 g] thinly sliced cabbage (green or red)

Juice of 1 lime, plus lime wedges for serving

Kosher salt

Freshly ground black pepper

¼ cup [50 g] pickled jalapeños, minced

¼ cup [35 g] minced white or yellow onion

1½ lb [680 g] white fish, such as cod, cut into 1 in [2.5 cm] pieces

¼ cup [35 g] cornstarch

¼ cup [35 g] all-purpose flour

1 Tbsp chili powder

1 cup [240 ml] neutral oil, such as grapeseed, or more as needed

12 corn tortillas

Hot sauce, for serving

Makes 4 servings • In a medium bowl, mash the chipotles in adobo into a rough paste with a fork. Add the mayonnaise and grated garlic and mix well. Set aside.

In another medium bowl, toss the cabbage with the lime juice and salt and pepper to taste. Set aside.

In a small bowl, mix together the jalapeños and onion. Set aside.

Season the fish with salt and pepper. In a wide, shallow bowl, whisk together the cornstarch, flour, chili powder, and plenty of salt and pepper.

In a large skillet over medium-high heat, warm the oil. It should be about ¼ in [6 mm] deep, just

enough to generously coat the skillet—you're not deep frying here. Dredge the fish in the flour mixture, shaking off any excess, and place it in the skillet. Be careful not to crowd the skillet; fry in as many batches as you need. Flip the fish after 3 to 4 minutes, once it's lightly golden on the first side, and fry the remaining side for another 3 minutes or so. Taste a piece of fish; if it needs more seasoning, add a bit more salt as it comes out of the skillet. Repeat with the remaining fish.

Meanwhile, in a medium pan over medium heat, warm the tortillas—30 seconds per side should do it. Wrap the tortillas in a kitchen towel to keep warm.

Set out the tortillas, fish, chipotle mayo, cabbage, onion-jalapeño mixture, and hot sauce to serve.

Grilling whole fish can seem intimidating, but it doesn't need to be. Arm yourself with a clean and hot grill, a flexible metal spatula, and plenty of salt, herbs, and lemon and you'll be pleasantly surprised. The fish will let you know when it's ready to be flipped—the skin will release easily from the grates. The earthy, spicy oregano is a great foil to the salty fish, especially when balanced out by the brightness of the lemon.

Whole Grilled Fish with Oregano and Lemon

Garlic Oregano Sauce

Peel of 2 lemons, thinly sliced

2 Tbsp oregano leaves

1 cup [20 g] parsley leaves

1 garlic clove

⅓ to ½ cup [80 to 120 ml] olive oil

Red pepper flakes

Kosher salt

Freshly ground black pepper

Grilled Fish

2 lemons, thinly sliced into rounds

8 oregano stems

4 whole fish, such as branzino or red snapper, gutted and scaled (have your fishmonger do it!)

Kosher salt

Freshly ground black pepper

¼ cup [60 ml] neutral oil, such as grapeseed

Makes 4 servings • **To make the garlic oregano sauce:** Place the lemon peel, oregano leaves, parsley leaves, and garlic clove on a cutting board. Finely chop all of the ingredients, mixing them together as you go, until everything seems uniformly finely chopped. Scrape the mixture into a small bowl and stir in ⅓ cup [80 ml] of olive oil, then more if needed. The sauce should be pourable but still thick with herbs. Add red pepper flakes to taste and season with salt and pepper. Set aside while you grill the fish.

To make the fish: Prepare a grill for medium-high heat. Divide the lemon slices and oregano stems among the fish and nestle them into the cavities. Season the insides with salt and pepper and tie

each fish closed with kitchen twine if you like—it's not necessary, but can be helpful. One firm knot around the thickest part of each fish will do. Season the exterior of the fish generously with salt and pepper and lightly coat them with the oil.

Place the fish on the grill and cook undisturbed for 8 to 10 minutes. Slide a flexible metal spatula under the fish and if they release fairly easily, flip them. They should have a lovely char to them; if not, raise the heat on the grill or let the second side cook on a hotter part of the grill. Cook for 8 to 10 minutes more, or until they release easily. Remove the twine, if using, and serve with the garlic oregano sauce.

This dish is so tasty and easy to put together! There are some really fancy canned fish products on the market nowadays, and that's what I would recommend using if you can find it. I like to drain the can of oil and put the fish in the fridge a few hours before making this salad, so that the fish tastes cold and fresh. Don't be shy on the salt for this one either—beans tend to absorb salt, so make sure you continue to taste and season as you go.

White Bean Salad with Fancy Tuna and Egg

1 garlic clove, grated

Zest and juice of 1 lemon

Kosher salt

4 eggs, at room temperature (see Note)

Two 15 oz [425 g] cans white beans, preferably navy or cannellini, drained and rinsed

¼ cup [60 ml] olive oil, plus more for serving

1 cup [20 g] mixed herbs, such as parsley, mint, cilantro, or dill, roughly chopped

One 6.7 oz [190 g] jar good-quality tuna packed in oil, such as Tonnino

Flaky sea salt, such as Maldon

Freshly ground black pepper

½ tsp red pepper flakes (optional)

Makes 4 servings • In a large bowl, mix together the garlic, lemon zest, and lemon juice. Add a large pinch of kosher salt, swirl the bowl to mix together, and set aside.

Bring a medium pot of water to a boil and carefully lower in the eggs. Boil for exactly 9 minutes, then immediately transfer the eggs to a bowl of ice water. Set aside.

Add the beans to the bowl with the garlic and lemon and stir to coat. Taste for salt and add more as needed. Let sit for 15 to 20 minutes. Add the olive oil and herbs and mix well. Drain the tuna if packed in oil, discard the oil, and gently fold the fish into the beans using a spoon. Taste for salt again—don't be afraid to season

liberally! Salt makes the difference between a bland bean and an absolutely delicious one.

Peel the eggs and slice them in half lengthwise.

Serve the bean salad in a large serving bowl or in individual bowls, topped with the egg halves. Drizzle olive oil over the eggs and season with flaky salt, black pepper, and red pepper flakes, if using.

Note. Room-temperature eggs are less likely to break and become misshapen while boiling. While you're at it, you might as well boil the remaining 8 eggs in the carton to have for snacks or to use in other recipes on your trip.

This tartine is chic. In recent years, smaller companies have really taken canned fish to another level. There are so many beautiful packaged options now! I like to collect fish tins during my travels to open on a rainy day when I want to make this toast.

Sardine Toast with Salted Butter, Mint, and Pickled Onion

2 slices good-quality bread, lightly toasted

4 to 6 Tbsp [55 to 85 g] salted butter, at room temperature

4 to 6 Tbsp [55 to 85 g] coarse ground mustard

1 tomato, thickly sliced

One 6.7 oz [190 g] tin sardines

Flaky sea salt

Freshly ground black pepper

¼ cup [40 g] Overnight Pickled Onions (page 61) or pickled vegetables of your choosing

8 to 10 mint leaves

Red pepper flakes (optional)

Makes 2 servings • Let the toasted bread cool, then generously spread the butter over the bread. Spread the mustard atop the butter, then top with sliced tomato. Divide the sardines between the bread slices and season with salt and pepper. Arrange the onions over the tops, tear the mint leaves, and sprinkle those over too. Top with red pepper flakes, if using, and serve.

How to Shop for Fish

I have been a pescatarian for over ten years, and I only eat fish on occasion. When I'm by the sea, however, I feel more inclined and inspired to cook fish. Since I eat it so infrequently, I'm picky with my fish. For example, I love a crab roll in the summer in Maine because I know that the stand where I go catches fresh crab daily. I try to stay away from the more popular fish that people like to cook with, such as tuna and salmon, since they are over-caught. I like fish with a milder taste, such as sea bass and sole, though I always like trying something different.

Go to a port or your local fishmonger to buy the freshest fish and to get the best advice. If you are shopping at a grocery store, I recommend going to a co-op and buying fresh, sustainable fish.

Sweet Finishes

This recipe is for my inner child. I grew up on tartine de Nutella, which is essentially toast topped with a chocolate hazelnut spread. This recipe is a slightly elevated version of that nostalgic and delicious treat. It's perfect for kids and grown-ups.

Salty Banana Nutella Toasts

¼ cup [50 g] light brown sugar

¼ cup [55 g] salted butter (see Note)

2 bananas

About ½ cup [190 g] Nutella

4 slices good-quality bread, toasted

Flaky sea salt

Makes 4 servings • Place a large cast-iron skillet over medium-high heat. Add the sugar and butter and stir until the sugar starts to melt, about 5 minutes—the mixture will start to bubble and look like it's caramelizing. Meanwhile, slice the bananas thinly on the bias, then add the slices to the skillet. Toss once, and then spread the bananas out evenly, with as little overlap as possible, so they can start to brown. Flip after about 5 minutes, or when the first side is beautifully golden brown, and cook for 4 to 5 minutes more. Transfer the bananas to a plate or shallow bowl when both sides are caramelized, and let cool for at least 5 minutes.

Meanwhile, spread the Nutella evenly on the four slices of toast, then top with the caramelized bananas and plenty of flaky salt.

Note. If you only have unsalted butter, just add a pinch of kosher salt to the sugar mixture.

Using the warm sun as a sous chef in this recipe is very fun. Once the tartine is assembled, I like to leave it on the hatch above the galley and let the sun do its thing. If you want to make it after sunset, simply place the toasts on a baking sheet and broil in the oven for 1 minute, or until the chocolate is just melted.

Sun-Melted Chocolate and Almond Butter Tartine

4 slices good-quality bread, toasted

¼ cup [60 ml] olive oil

½ cup [170 g] creamy almond butter

2 oz [55 g] dark chocolate

Flaky sea salt

Makes 4 servings • Drizzle the toasted bread with the olive oil. Spread the almond butter evenly on the four slices. Break the chocolate into small chunks and scatter it over the almond butter. Place the toasts on a large plate or baking sheet and set in a sunny spot on a hot day, until the chocolate melts, about 10 to 15 minutes, depending on how hot it is outside. Swirl it with a butter knife, if you wish, and sprinkle with flaky salt. Enjoy immediately.

This dessert is for adults only! These spiked sherbet cups make for a fun presentation. You can serve them on a big plate and get creative with the garnishes (paper umbrellas would be fun!). Tell your friends to not be shy and dig in, as these cups melt quickly.

Campari Sherbet Cups

4 navel oranges

½ cup [120 ml] coconut cream (see Note)

One 15 oz [425 g] can cream of coconut (such as Coco Lopez)

2 Tbsp lime juice

2 Tbsp Campari

½ tsp kosher salt

Makes 8 servings • Halve the oranges crosswise and run a paring knife along the interior of the peel to loosen the edges of the segments. Use a spoon to scoop out all the segments, placing the juicy bits of orange in a medium bowl. You should be left with eight neat little cups, which can be arranged on a 9 by 13 in [23 by 33 cm] rimmed baking sheet (or similar size baking dish), wedged together so they're in an upright position.

Place the coconut cream in a high-powered blender and mix on medium speed for 1 to 2 minutes, or until the cream is aerated and smooth. Squeeze the orange segments in the bowl to release ¼ cup [60 ml] of juice (save the rest of the juice and orange segments for another use, if you like) and add the orange juice to the blender with the cream of coconut, lime juice, Campari, and salt. Blend on medium speed for about 30 seconds, or until the mixture is very smooth.

Let the contents of the blender settle for a minute or so, tapping it on the counter a few times to release some air bubbles. Pour the mixture into the orange cups. Carefully transfer the baking sheet to the freezer and freeze the cups for at least 4 hours and up to overnight. Serve as is with spoons, or slice them into wedges and eat immediately with your hands.

Note. Coconut cream and cream of coconut are not the same thing—cream of coconut is much sweeter. If you can only find coconut milk, make your own coconut cream: Place a can of full-fat coconut milk, ideally with no gums or stabilizers, in the refrigerator overnight. The next day, flip it upside down, open the can, and scoop out the solid coconut cream. Pour the remaining coconut water on ice for a drink, or reserve for another use.

If you feel like being a bit naughty, top these with a little whipped cream.

Lemon Tahini Cookies

¾ cup [150 g] granulated sugar

Zest of 1 lemon, finely chopped

2 cups [280 g] all-purpose flour

1 tsp baking powder

¾ tsp kosher salt

¾ cup [170 g] unsalted butter, at room temperature

1 egg

¾ cup [220 g] tahini

¼ cup [35 g] sesame seeds, toasted

¼ cup [50 g] turbinado sugar

Makes 18 cookies • In a medium bowl, mix together the granulated sugar and lemon zest, pinching the zest with your fingers until it is completely incorporated and the sugar is fragrant. Set aside.

In another medium bowl, whisk together the flour, baking powder, and salt. Set aside.

Add the butter to the bowl with the lemon sugar and mix by hand or with a hand mixer on high speed until pale and fluffy, 10 to 12 minutes by hand or 6 minutes with a hand mixer, scraping the bowl with a rubber spatula once or twice. Add the egg and mix on low speed for 1 minute, scraping the bowl again. Add the tahini and mix on low speed for 30 seconds or until smooth. Add the flour mixture and fold it in with a rubber spatula until no dry spots remain.

Transfer the mixture to a large piece of parchment paper or plastic wrap and form it into a log about 10 in [25 cm] long, then roll it up tightly. Refrigerate for at least 4 hours, or overnight.

Preheat the oven to 350°F [180°C]. On a wide plate, mix together the sesame seeds and turbinado sugar. Unwrap the dough and roll it in the seed mixture, pressing so the mixture adheres well. Cut the dough with a sharp knife into slices about ⅓ in [8.5 mm] thick; you should get about 18 cookies. Place them on a cookie sheet with a Silpat liner or parchment paper underneath, and bake for 16 to 18 minutes, or until the edges are golden, the sesame seeds are fragrant, and they feel almost firm and dry to the touch. (Check halfway through baking, and if they are browning unevenly, rotate the pan.) They'll continue to firm up as they cool. Store covered, unrefrigerated, for up to 1 week.

I fortunately have never felt sick on a boat, but many friends have. These cookies will settle your stomach, and they are great paired with tea. (If you feel queasy, ginger is your friend. I had a ginger candy in my mouth my whole first trimester while I was pregnant with my daughter, Romy.)

Oat Digestive Cookies

2 cups [200 g] old-fashioned oats

¼ cup [50 g] granulated sugar

2 Tbsp ground flax

1 Tbsp ground ginger

1½ tsp kosher salt

½ tsp baking soda

½ cup [113 g] chilled unsalted butter, cut into pieces (see Note)

¼ cup [60 ml] milk

¼ cup [35 g] all-purpose or oat flour, for rolling

Makes 16 cookies • In a blender or food processor, finely grind the oats to a powder. This will take anywhere from 1 to 5 minutes, depending on the strength of your machine. (Or use 1¾ cups [210 g] of store-bought oat flour.) Add the sugar, flax, ginger, salt, and baking soda to the blender and pulse to combine. Add the cold butter and pulse until the mixture resembles coarse meal and there are no large pieces of butter remaining. Dump the contents into a large bowl and chill for at least 30 minutes, or overnight.

Preheat the oven to 325°F [165°C]. Remove the oat mixture from the fridge and add the milk. Gently stir with a wooden spoon, or better yet, mix with your hands, until the mixture just comes together. Turn it out onto a clean work surface and knead briefly until the dough is well combined and no dry spots remain, about 3 minutes. Lightly flour the work surface and roll the dough to ¼ in [6 mm] thickness. Cut out cookies with a 2 in [5 cm] diameter cookie cutter, lightly flouring the cutter to avoid sticking, and place the cookies on a baking sheet lined with parchment paper. Bring the scraps together, lightly knead, roll it out again, and cut out more cookies until no dough remains.

Prick the cookies all over with the tines of a fork, then bake for 16 to 18 minutes, rotating the pan halfway through, or until the edges and bottoms of the cookies are lightly golden. Let cool and store for up to 5 days in a tightly sealed container.

Note. For a vegan option, you can easily substitute vegan butter and plant-based milk in this recipe.

It might sound a bit *romantic* to devote time toward *creating* a relationship with *the sea*. When you learn to *love something*, you observe, pay attention to it, and *share experiences* together. You build a connection while learning to *flow* with the ups and downs—the *waves* of what comes with being *alive* (pun intended). I invite you to try and tap into these *feelings* with the sea, if you have not already.

Enjoy this compote alone, on toast or plain yogurt for breakfast, or with Chia Pudding (page 42) for dessert. If cherries are not in season, you can use frozen cherries.

Cherry Compote with Bitters and Ginger

1 lb [455 g] cherries, pitted

2 Tbsp granulated sugar

1 in [2.5 cm] piece of ginger, grated

1 Tbsp lemon juice

1 tsp bitters

Makes 8 to 10 servings • Combine all of the ingredients in a medium heavy-bottomed pot and bring to a simmer over medium heat. Cook for 1 to 1½ hours, or until the cherries have become soft and the liquid they release is reduced, thickened, and jammy. If you'd like to test it, put a small plate in the freezer for 15 minutes or so, then dollop a spoonful of compote onto the chilled plate—if it sets up like jam, it's done. If it's still very runny, you can cook it a bit longer. Let cool and store it in the fridge for up to 1 month.

This recipe is great in the summer when your kitchen is abundant with berries and you are trying to think of what to do with them all. Nowadays, my little family tries to spend most of the summers in mid-coast Maine and the berries—especially the wild blueberries—are absolutely divine, but they come and go quickly. I love making this crumble right before I see the berries turn and enjoying it outside under the stars. Top each serving with crème fraîche if you have it, or Greek yogurt.

Gingery Berry Crisp with Granola Crumble

Filling

2 lb [910 g] mixed fresh berries, such as blueberries, raspberries, blackberries, or strawberries

¼ to ½ cup [50 to 100 g] granulated sugar, depending on the sweetness of your fruit

2 Tbsp all-purpose flour

1 tsp fresh grated ginger

½ tsp kosher salt

Juice of 1 lemon

Crumble Topping

¾ cup [105 g] all-purpose flour

6 Tbsp [85 g] unsalted butter, melted

6 Tbsp [90 g] light brown sugar

¾ tsp kosher salt

2 cups [190 g] granola

Makes 6 to 8 servings • **To make the filling:** Preheat the oven to 350°F [180°C]. In a large bowl, mix together the berries, granulated sugar, flour, ginger, salt, and lemon juice. Pour the fruit into a 10 in [25 cm] cast-iron skillet, 1 qt [945 ml] casserole dish, or pie pan.

To make the crumble topping: In the same bowl, mix together the flour, butter, brown sugar, salt, and granola. Use your hands to squeeze the ingredients together until no floury bits remain.

Sprinkle the crumble evenly over the fruit filling and bake for 45 to 55 minutes, or until the crumble is deeply golden brown and the fruit is bubbling thickly. Let cool before serving. Keep leftovers tightly covered in the refrigerator for up to 3 days.

I have tried to make chocolate mousse on boats a few times, but I usually end up standing in the galley in my bathing suit beating the eggs for 15 minutes to little avail. Eventually I gave up trying. With this recipe, you get the satisfaction of a chocolate mousse without the struggle! It's an indulgent dessert that remains light. You can make a few extra pots to keep in the fridge for a few days in case a sudden craving comes on.

Pot de Crème au Chocolat with Lemon Whipped Cream

Chocolate Mousse

1 cup [240 g] full-fat yogurt

½ tsp salt

8 oz [230 g] dark chocolate, roughly chopped

¾ cup [180 ml] milk

Lemon Whipped Cream

1 cup [240 ml] heavy whipping cream

1 Tbsp granulated sugar

Zest and juice of 1 lemon

Makes 4 servings • **To make the chocolate mousse:** In a large bowl, whisk together the yogurt and salt until smooth.

In a medium heatproof bowl, add the chopped chocolate, reserving about 2 Tbsp of the fine dusty bits to use for garnish. In a small pot over low heat, warm the milk until bubbles just begin to form on the edges; be sure not to let it boil. Pour the warm milk over the chocolate, swirling the bowl until the chocolate is submerged. Let sit for 2 to 3 minutes, then gently whisk the milk and chocolate together until completely smooth. If the milk cools too quickly and some pieces of chocolate remain, put 1 in [2.5 cm] of water in the small pot, bring to a simmer, and place the bowl with the chocolate and milk over it, making sure the bowl doesn't touch the water, creating a double boiler. Continuously whisk until the ganache is completely smooth and shiny.

Pour the chocolate ganache into the large bowl with the yogurt and salt and, switching to a rubber spatula, fold the ganache into the yogurt until smooth. Divide the mixture evenly among four 8 oz [240 ml] mason jars or other small vessels. Let chill in the refrigerator for at least 1 hour, or overnight.

To make the lemon whipped cream: Pour the cream into a large mixing bowl. Beat with a whisk until soft peaks begin to form, 8 to 10 minutes. Add the sugar, lemon zest, and lemon juice, and whisk gently until soft peaks form.

To serve: Spoon a little whipped cream over each vessel of chocolate mousse, then sprinkle with a bit of the reserved chocolate dust.

Apricots in the summer are the best! I made this cobbler on a sailing trip in Greece—I think we were on our way to Hydra. It was so delicious that it lasted all of 5 minutes. Warm, fresh apricots also smell *so good*. If you can't find apricots, any stone fruit (like peaches!) can work here.

Lazy Apricot Cobbler

Fruit Filling

¼ cup [55 g] unsalted butter

6 cups sliced fresh apricots (about 3 lb [1.4 kg] before slicing)

¼ to ½ cup [50 to 100 g] granulated sugar, depending on sweetness

Juice of 1 lemon (or 1 tsp apple cider vinegar)

½ tsp kosher salt

1 Tbsp cornstarch

Cobbler Topping

2 cups [280 g] all-purpose flour

2 Tbsp sugar, plus more for sprinkling

1½ tsp baking powder

1 tsp cinnamon

1 tsp kosher salt

½ cup [113 g] unsalted butter, melted

¾ cup [180 ml] milk

½ tsp flaky sea salt

Whipped Cream

1 cup [240 ml] heavy cream

2 Tbsp granulated sugar

Pinch of kosher salt

Makes 6 to 8 servings • Preheat the oven to 375°F [190°C].

To make the fruit filling: In a 10 in [25 cm] cast-iron skillet over medium heat, melt the butter and cook until browned and nutty smelling, about 8 minutes (you'll have to go by smell because you can't see the browning against the dark skillet). Remove from the heat.

In a large bowl, mix together the apricots, sugar, lemon juice, kosher salt, and cornstarch until well combined. Add the fruit to the skillet, mix gently to combine, then bake for 15 minutes.

To make the cobbler topping: In a large bowl, mix together the flour, sugar, baking powder, cinnamon, and kosher salt. Pour the melted butter and milk into the dry ingredients and mix until just combined. Let rest while the fruit bakes.

After the fruit has baked for 15 minutes, delicately tear the dough into rough chunks and place it on top of the apricots, nestling it into the fruit. Sprinkle the dough with sugar and flaky salt and bake for 30 to 35 minutes more, or until the fruit is bubbling thickly and the topping is deeply golden brown.

To make the whipped cream: Place a large bowl in the freezer. When it's very cold, pour the heavy cream in and start whisking. When it starts to thicken, add the sugar and a pinch of kosher salt. Continue whisking until you've reached soft peaks. Serve the warm cobbler with the whipped cream.

The absolute best surprise is when you forget you've made this skillet brownie, discover it late at night, and enjoy it with a glass of wine such as Pedro Ximénez (I know, very specific) or a sweet sherry wine. That is the ultimate nightcap.

Brown Butter Cornmeal Brownie in a Cast-Iron Skillet

1 cup [226 g] unsalted butter

1½ cups [120 g] cocoa powder

½ cup [70 g] cornmeal

¾ tsp kosher salt

½ tsp cinnamon

4 eggs

1 cup [200 g] granulated sugar

1 cup [200 g] light brown sugar

1 tsp vanilla extract

Makes 6 to 8 servings • Preheat the oven to 300°F [150°C]. In a 10 in [25 cm] cast-iron skillet over medium heat, melt the butter and cook until browned and nutty smelling, 10 to 15 minutes. Pour the brown butter into a glass bowl or measuring cup and set aside to cool, reserving the buttery pan.

Meanwhile, in a medium bowl, whisk together the cocoa powder, cornmeal, salt, and cinnamon. Set aside.

In a large bowl, whisk together the eggs, granulated sugar, brown sugar, and vanilla until frothy and well combined, about 3 minutes. Whisk in the brown butter, then fold in the dry ingredients until just combined.

Return the skillet to medium heat, and once it's hot, scrape in the brownie batter. Transfer to the oven and bake for 35 to 40 minutes, or until a toothpick inserted comes out clean, with just a few crumbs. Let cool for at least 1 hour, invert from the pan, and serve.

Buckwheat is kind of a funky flour. It makes this bread look dark in color and gives it a nutty flavor. If you can't find buckwheat while shopping, don't sweat it, just substitute with regular flour in equal measure. The buckwheat makes it special though, so if you can find it, give it a try for a unique take on banana bread.

Buckwheat Chocolate Banana Bread

⅓ cup [80 ml] olive oil, plus more for greasing the pan

2 cups [280 g] all-purpose flour

½ cup [70 g] buckwheat flour

1 tsp baking soda

1 tsp kosher salt

½ tsp ground cardamom

½ cup [120 ml] maple syrup

¼ cup [60 g] full-fat yogurt

3 eggs

3 very ripe bananas, mashed

4 oz [115 g] bittersweet chocolate, chopped

1 Tbsp cane sugar, for topping

½ tsp flaky sea salt, for topping

Makes 8 servings • Preheat the oven to 325°F [165°C]. Brush a 9 by 5 in [23 by 13 cm] loaf pan with olive oil and line the long sides and base with a single piece of parchment paper.

In a large bowl, whisk together the flours, baking soda, kosher salt, and cardamom.

In a separate large bowl, whisk together the maple syrup, ⅓ cup [80 ml] olive oil, yogurt, eggs, and bananas. With a rubber spatula, fold the dry ingredients into the wet ingredients, mixing until just combined. Fold in the chopped chocolate.

Scrape the mixture into the prepared pan and sprinkle with the cane sugar and flaky salt. Bake for 55 to 60 minutes, rotating the pan once halfway through, or until a toothpick or butter knife inserted into the center comes out clean with just a few crumbs sticking to it. Let cool completely before serving, inverting onto a wire rack after 20 minutes, if you like.

This cake is gluten free, y'all! It's also straightforward to make and not too sweet, so you can eat it at any time of day. When baking on a boat, it's best to keep things simple so you don't need to worry about your oven and its ability to bake in a precise way. This cake is no frills, but it's still so impressive when you whip up a cake in the galley on your way to your next spot.

Orange Cardamom Almond Cake

½ cup [120 ml] olive oil, plus more for greasing the pan

3 cups [380 g] natural almond flour (see Note)

1 Tbsp ground cardamom

2½ tsp baking powder

1½ tsp kosher salt, plus more for the candied rind

3 oranges

3 eggs

1 cup [200 g] granulated sugar, plus more for the candied rind

Thick full-fat yogurt or unsweetened whipped cream, for serving

Makes 8 servings • Preheat the oven to 325°F [165°C]. Grease a 9 in [23 cm] cake pan with a bit of olive oil and set aside.

In a large bowl, mix together the almond flour, cardamom, baking powder, and salt and set aside.

Zest 2 of the oranges with a Microplane and place the oranges in a separate large bowl. Remove wide strips of rind from the remaining orange with a vegetable peeler and set aside. Juice all three oranges into the bowl with the zest. Add the eggs and ½ cup [100 g] of the sugar and whisk until smooth. Add the ½ cup [120 ml] of olive oil and whisk to incorporate. Pour the wet mixture into the dry mixture and stir with a wooden spoon or rubber spatula until smooth.

Transfer the batter to the prepared pan and bake for about 45 minutes, rotating once, or until the cake is starting to darken around the edges and a toothpick inserted into the center comes out clean with just a few crumbs. Let cool completely, then unmold from the pan.

Meanwhile, in a medium pan over medium-high heat, bring the remaining ½ cup [100 g] of sugar and ½ cup [120 ml] of water to a boil, then lower the heat and simmer. Very thinly slice the orange rind strips into long ribbons. Simmer in the syrup for about 8 minutes, until soft and the bitterness has mellowed. Lift the strips out of the syrup and drain on a paper towel or paper bag, reserving the syrup. Sprinkle a few Tbsp of sugar and a big pinch of salt on a small plate and swirl to mix. When the candied rind is cool, toss it in the sugar-salt mixture.

When the cake is cool, lightly brush a bit of the syrup over the top (not too much or it will affect the texture of the cake—you're just looking for a slight sheen). Arrange the candied zest over the top. Serve with Greek yogurt.

Note. You can grind your own raw almonds (14 oz [400 g]) in a food processor if you like, but they should be very finely ground. I like skin-on for flavor and texture.

A cake with a candle goes a long way, and this cake is so easy to whip up, you'll use any occasion as an excuse to make it (your dog's birthday counts!). Pro tip: Take a pack of cute candles with you on trips. It's a little thing, but that's the kind of detail that really changes the vibe and impresses your guests.

Birthday Cake (or, Chocolate Olive Oil Loaf Cake)

Cake

¾ cup [180 ml] olive oil, plus more for greasing the pan

1 cup [140 g] all-purpose flour

½ cup [40 g] cocoa powder

½ cup [100 g] light brown sugar

½ cup [100 g] cane sugar

3 eggs

2 tsp vanilla extract

1 tsp kosher salt

½ tsp baking soda

½ cup [120 ml] hot coffee

Glaze

½ cup [120 g] full-fat yogurt

¼ cup [30 g] confectioners' sugar

¼ tsp kosher salt

Makes 8 servings • **To make the cake:** Preheat the oven to 325°F [165°C]. Grease a 9 by 5 in [23 by 13 cm] loaf pan or half-size Pullman pan with a bit of olive oil and line the long sides and bottom with a single piece of parchment paper.

In a large bowl, whisk together the flour and cocoa powder, then set aside.

In a large bowl, combine the ¾ cup [180 ml] of olive oil, brown sugar, cane sugar, eggs, vanilla, salt, and baking soda. Whisk vigorously for about 3 minutes. Fold the dry ingredients into the wet ingredients, then gently mix in the hot coffee, combining thoroughly—it takes a minute or so to integrate the coffee completely.

Transfer the batter to the prepared pan and bake the cake for about 60 minutes, rotating once halfway through, or until a toothpick or butter knife inserted comes out clean. Let cool completely, inverting the cake onto a wire rack after about 20 minutes, if you like.

To make the glaze: In a large bowl, whisk together the yogurt, confectioners' sugar, and salt until very smooth. When the cake is fully cool, spoon the glaze over the top, letting it run down the sides.

The Magic of Coconuts

Coconuts are like avocados: delicious, filling, and chock-full of the good fats that keep your body running like a well-oiled machine. Not only is the water of a coconut more hydrating than regular water because of its electrolyte component, but the meat is healing and nourishing. It is as close to human plasma as we can find in nature. Vitamins A, D, and B_{12}; calcium; protein; healthy carbs; and minerals can be found in this incredible fruit. Coconut meat can be eaten with a spoon or used in a salad; the milk has myriad uses, from coffee (see page 34) to oats (see page 47) to ceviche (see page 121).

On page 20, I mention that coconut oil is one of my pantry essentials. Not only can the oil be used for cooking in high heat, but it is a killer moisturizer, antifungal, and natural SPF 7. It can also be used for "oil pulling." In the morning, take a swig of coconut oil in your mouth and swoosh it around for 5 to 10 minutes. (Be sure to spit it out when you're through!) This is an Ayurvedic practice that can reinforce your gums, kill bad germs, and naturally whiten teeth.

If you find yourself sailing somewhere tropical, get your share of this golden ingredient to stay hydrated and heal yourself on the inside and the outside.

Acknowledgments

I feel privileged and grateful that I got the opportunity to sail in so many different parts of the world and have these memories to cherish while I was simultaneously trying to find a bit of myself in my thirties. The Sailing Collective is such an amazing company, and I hope they know how thankful I am for the opportunity they have given me and the experiences I received on all my trips.

In this book, I have partnered with my friend and wonderful chef Laura, who has helped me make sure these recipes translate from my headspace to paper! She is so talented in the kitchen, and I believe she and I share a similar ethos when it comes to cooking: Keep dishes simple yet delicious, and pour a lot of love into them.

I started writing this book before the pandemic and before having a baby. I am so grateful to Laura for keeping me going to finish this project through the lack of sleep and hurdles that came along the past few years in the journey of writing this book. But most important, I am so thankful that she believed in my story and shared her talent and skills with me to create these recipes. This book is as much hers as it is mine.

This book fills me with memories of adventure, love, and so much swimming. Now that I am a mom, I hope my daughter, Romy, can read this book one day and feel inspired to create her own experiences. I didn't know I could love anything more than the ocean, but Romy, I was wrong. I love you, my sweet baby.

I am so thankful for Meg Thompson, my literary agent, who years ago believed in my story more than I believed in myself at the time. I feel honored to be in the roster of books that have been published under her name.

I wouldn't have been able to make this book a reality if it wasn't for my kind husband, Devin, who helped me find time to write this book and tested all the recipes the past few years, making sure they were tasty. I love you, and I hope we have many adventures by the ocean together with our little family until our hair turns gray.

Index

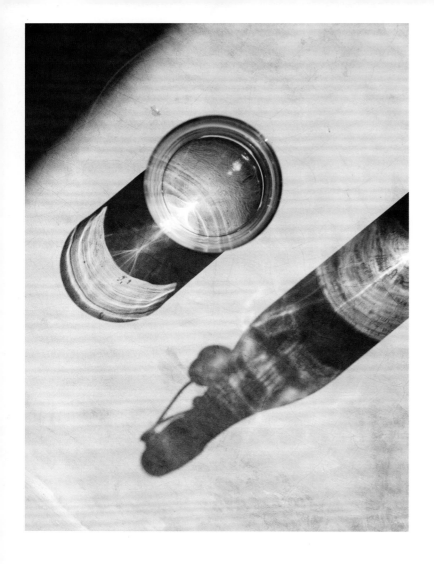